WELL, YOU DID ASK

Why the UK voted to leave the EU

Michael Ashcroft & Kevin Culwick

Biteback Publishing

First published in Great Britain in 2016 by
Biteback Publishing Ltd
Westminster Tower
3 Albert Embankment
London SE1 7SP
Copyright © Michael Ashcroft and Kevin Culwick 2016

ISBN 978-1-78590-168-3

10 9 8 7 6 5 4 3 2 1

A CIP catalogue record for this book is available
from the British Library.

Set in Adobe Caslon Pro by Adrian McLaughlin

Printed and bound in Great Britain by
CPI Group (UK) Ltd, Croydon CR0 4YY

CONTENTS

ABOUT THE AUTHORS

Lord Ashcroft KCMG PC is an international businessman, author and philanthropist. He is founder and chairman of the board of Crimestoppers, a member of the board of the Imperial War Museum and a trustee of the Imperial War Museum Foundation, chairman of the Trustees of Ashcroft Technology Academy, chancellor of Anglia Ruskin University and treasurer of the International Democrat Union. From 2005 to 2010 he was deputy chairman of the Conservative Party. His political works include *Smell the Coffee: A Wake-Up Call for the Conservative Party*; *Minority Verdict*; *Project Blueprint*; *What Future for Labour?*; *What Are the Liberal Democrats For?*; *It's Not You, It's Them: Research to Remind Politicians What Matters*; *Degrees of Separation: Ethnic Minority Voters and the Conservative Party*; *They're Thinking What We're Thinking: Understanding the UKIP Temptation*; *Small Island: Public Opinion and the Politics of Immigration*; *Europe on Trial*; *Cameron's Caledonian Conundrum*; *Project Red Dawn: Labour's Revival (And Survival)*; *Pay Me Forty Quid and I'll Tell You: The 2015 Election Campaign through the Eyes of the Voters* (with Kevin Culwick); *The Unexpected Mandate: The 2015 Election, the Parties, the People – and the Future*; and *Call Me Dave: The Unauthorised Biography of David Cameron* (with Isabel Oakeshott). His research is published at LordAshcroftPolls.com.

Kevin Culwick has been the director of Lord Ashcroft Polls since 2010. He was formerly head of opinion research for the

Conservative Party, having previously worked in the polling industry and in politics. He is the co-author of *Pay Me Forty Quid and I'll Tell You: The 2015 Election Campaign through the Eyes of the Voters* (with Michael Ashcroft).

INTRODUCTION
Lord Ashcroft KCMG PC

I supported Brexit. In an article two days before the referendum, I argued that history has shown the European Union to be not so much an organisation as a process. By deciding to remain, I felt, Britain would not be opting for the status quo but tying itself to a body whose ambitions were very different from our own.

But this book is not about my views. Nor is it an inside account of the campaign and its protagonists.

Instead, we have tried to tell the story of the EU referendum from the point of view of its most important participants, the voters. And it is a remarkable story. A question that was of only passing interest to most people in Britain turned into what David Cameron called "a once in a generation moment to shape the destiny of our country" and, ultimately, perhaps the most momentous political decision of our time.

For many people, this was an uncomfortable journey. As I argued in *Pay Me Forty Quid and I'll Tell You: The 2015 Election Campaign through the Eyes of the Voters*, there is a wisdom to the electorate that should not be underestimated. But large numbers of people found it harder to decide between leaving and remaining in the EU than to choose a government at a general election. Picking a group of people who more or less look as though they are up to making big policy decisions is easier, they quickly realised, than making those decisions themselves.

Many found they were floating voters, a role to which they were unaccustomed.

I think there are three main reasons why so many found the choice so taxing. The first is that the two options did not come with convenient party labels. Though people grumble about partisan politics, the parties' competing brands – their familiar character, principles, policies and personalities, and their history in or out of office – help voters make decisions. With their usual party divided, or with politicians they would usually disagree with suspiciously backing the outcome they felt most drawn towards, many felt at sea.

The second reason is that people hoped they would be furnished with a battery of useful facts to guide their thinking, but no such facts arrived, or, at least, none they could rely on. Voters questioned every forecast about the consequences of Brexit, good or bad. But if predictions about the future were inevitably up for debate, so, to their exasperation, were statements about the present, such as how much Britain paid into the EU budget each year. The decision seemed more important than those they made at elections, when they could change their mind after five years, but voters felt much less equipped to make it.

The third reason is that the rival campaigns, by indulging in hyperbole, obscured rather than clarified the issues at stake, making it harder for voters to get to the bottom of what really mattered. Warnings of the catastrophe that would ensue from making the wrong decision (especially from the remain campaign) seemed overblown, and the motives of the main players (especially on the leave side) seemed mixed, at best.

For two and a half years, Lord Ashcroft Polls looked in depth at how British voters saw their country's relationship with Europe, and how they would approach the question in a referendum. In the weeks leading up to David Cameron's Brussels renegotiation – an episode which arguably did as much to draw attention to the drawbacks of membership as it did to highlight the UK's new "special status" – we polled people in the twenty-seven other member states on their attitude to Europe and, crucially, to Britain. In a unique exercise, we visited ten EU capitals to report in more detail what voters throughout the continent made of the UK's attitude to Europe and what concessions, if any, they were prepared for their leaders to make to keep us on board. For nine weeks leading to polling day, we conducted focus groups in every region of the UK to see what undecided voters were making of the campaign, its personalities, its claims and counterclaims, the barrage of figures (if not exactly facts) and the battalions of experts wheeled out to enlighten them. Finally, on referendum day itself, we surveyed more than twelve thousand people to find out who had voted to stay and who had voted to go, and what had persuaded them.

All of that research is collected here. It reveals a number of important things beyond what people thought about Britain's relationship with the EU. One is that both the remain and the leave camps were coalitions of voters, not monoliths. Each side attracted people with different backgrounds and priorities. On the leave side, the affluent *Global Britain* segment of the electorate we identified from our polling had little in common with those in the *Nothing to Lose* group; among remainers, the paths of the *I'm Alright, Jacques* and *If It Ain't Broke* voters would rarely cross.

Another is that, for many voters, the decision was only tangentially related to Europe at all. At least as powerful were how people saw the world, and their place in it. Some did not want the question put before the country in the first place,

PROLOGUE: A NATION SHRUGS

"I don't want to be the sort of person
who has views about Europe."
Focus group participant, London, March 2014

On 23 January 2013, David Cameron announced that he would, were he returned to Downing Street at the general election, hold an in–out referendum on his country's membership of the European Union.

> The next Conservative Manifesto in 2015 will ask for a mandate from the British people for a Conservative government to negotiate a new settlement with our European partners in the next parliament. It will be a relationship with the Single Market at its heart. And when we have negotiated that new settlement, we will give the British people a referendum with a very simple in-or-out choice. To stay in the EU on these new terms; or come out altogether.

The announcement that a great national question will finally be put to the people usually represents a major accomplishment for a political leader. Two years earlier, the country had given its verdict (albeit a decisively unfavourable one) on electoral reform. The vote was the culmination of decades of campaigning by the Liberal Democrats and their predecessors – a personal achievement, if not exactly a victory, for the Deputy Prime Minister, Nick Clegg. Two months later, Alex Salmond, the First Minister of Scotland, would announce the date of the referendum on Scottish independence to which he had devoted his political life.

But for Cameron, the declaration was not an achievement but a concession. Only fifteen months earlier, Conservative MPs had been whipped to oppose a motion, proposed by the Tory backbencher David Nuttall, calling for a referendum in which the public would choose between the status quo, reforming the terms of the UK's membership, or leaving altogether. Eighty-one Tories defied the whip, making it the biggest rebellion ever against a Conservative Prime Minister over Europe. Some argued that Tories should have been allowed a free vote, since opposition from Labour and the Lib Dems would ensure there was no danger of the motion being carried, but Downing Street was unrepentant. As a spokesman for the PM put it after the result:

> The government has to do what is in the national interest. The easy thing to do would have been for us to have avoided expressing a view. It was important to take a strong lead – because Britain's best interests are served by being in the EU.

In June 2012, more than one hundred Conservative MPs signed a letter demanding legislation for a referendum after the following election. Questioned by reporters at a summit in Brussels, Cameron said that he wanted to see powers returning from Brussels, that Europe was evolving and that he was "an optimist about getting this relationship right". The problem with an in–out referendum, he added, was that "it actually only gives people those two choices: you can either stay in, with all the status quo, or you can get out".

Now the Prime Minister had pledged the referendum that it had been "in the national interest" to oppose. In doing so he made a virtue of necessity – the necessity of keeping together his parliamentary party.

For some Conservatives, the preoccupation with Europe that brought John Major's government to the brink of collapse in 1993 had never really gone away, and Cameron had never been able to satisfy them. A number of his MPs resented the decision, made in opposition in 2009, to admit that a future Tory government would be unable to hold a referendum on the Lisbon Treaty since it had by then been ratified by every EU member state. In October 2012, after the European Commission proposed a 5 per cent increase in the EU budget, Tory MPs publicly demanded that Cameron secure a cut, while the PM himself thought a freeze was the best that was likely to be achieved. Fifty-three Conservatives defied the whip when the matter came to a vote in Parliament.

The fixation with Europe was bolstered by the "UKIP threat" which had, by this time, come to obsess many Tories. Despite coming second in the European election of 2009, at the general election of the following year the UK Independence Party won just 3 per cent of the vote. But two years into the coalition government, UKIP had drawn level in the polls with the Lib Dems, and by the autumn of 2012 was regularly scoring into double figures. UKIP came second in two parliamentary by-elections, in Rotherham and Middlesbrough, prompting its leader Nigel Farage to declare that his party was "the new third force in British politics".

Surveys at the time suggested new UKIP supporters were coming disproportionately from the Conservatives. With

Labour ahead and many Tories wondering whether they would keep their seats, let alone remain in government, demand grew for Cameron to do something that might stifle UKIP's appeal. A referendum on Europe was, for some, the obvious response.

Yet, despite the party's name, people's attraction to UKIP owed more to their outlook and their distrust of mainstream politicians than to any policy. As Lord Ashcroft Polls found at the end of 2012, only just over a quarter of voters saying they were considering UKIP said that resolving Britain's future relations with the EU was among the top three issues facing the country; only 7 per cent of them said it was the most important of all. Economic growth and jobs, welfare reform, immigration and the deficit all mattered to them more.

For those reasons, whatever its merits as a policy, the pledge to renegotiate Britain's relationship with the EU and put the result before the people in a referendum was never likely to halt the rise of UKIP: within weeks of Cameron's announcement UKIP had moved comfortably into third place, regularly recording poll shares in the mid or even high teens. The party won 23 per cent of the vote in the May 2013 local elections, just two points behind the Tories.

Whether this surprised those who argued for a referendum as a way of shooting UKIP's fox is unclear. There was, after all, a convenient link between apparent electoral expedience and the policy they wanted anyway. It was perhaps notable that in the mid-1990s, with Tory councils and parliamentary seats toppling to the Lib Dems, the argument was seldom to be heard that the Major government should take a leaf out of the Lib Dem book and promise to join the euro or put a penny on income tax. Either way, by the end of 2012, Cameron had decided that a continuing row over Europe would distract from his wider mission and the task of winning a majority: clearly, the rebels would not give him a moment's peace until he gave them what they wanted.

When it came to Europe, the real distinction between Cameron and many others in the Conservative Party was not his position but his fervour, or lack of it. Part of this was deliberate. In standing for the leadership, Cameron had set out to modernise his party, which, more than a decade after the rebellions over the Maastricht Treaty, had never completely expunged its reputation for "banging on about Europe", as he often put it. (Not that it had tried very hard: as recently as 2001 its general election campaign had been dominated by its call to "keep the pound", a rallying cry often, literally, issued through a megaphone from the back of a truck. Tony Blair, meanwhile, was seen every day in a school or hospital. The public interpreted the parties' priorities from these visual cues and voted accordingly. The fact that Labour had in any case promised a referendum on any decision for Britain to join the euro made the Tories' choice of theme all the more eccentric.) Cameron was determined to change the subject.

But there was a second reason why Cameron never showed much zeal on the European question: he simply didn't think it was very interesting or, in the great scheme of things, all that important. Iain Duncan Smith, his Work and Pensions Secretary and a predecessor as Tory leader, observed:

> If you asked him instinctively, how much of what the EU does do you think is good, I think the answer would probably be not much. Does he think it's worth having huge bust-ups and fights over? No.

Cameron himself had always considered himself a Eurosceptic. As a prospective Conservative candidate in 2000, he insisted in a series of emails to Sean Gabb, proprietor of the Candidlist website that classified Tory hopefuls according to their stance on Europe, that he should be identified as a sceptic. Gabb was initially unconvinced, musing that Cameron might more accurately be labelled a Europhile. He eventually relented and designated him a "sceptic" after Cameron protested that his views were clear:

> No to the single currency, no to further transfer of powers from Westminster to Brussels and yes to renegotiation of areas like fish where the EU has been a disaster for the UK. If that is being a Europhile, then I'm a banana.
>
> For the last thirty years politicians have given up far too much sovereignty and explained far too little about the true nature of European institutions. This issue is one of the reasons I want to stand for Parliament in the first place.

Early Cameron

As Tory leader, Cameron withdrew the Conservatives in the European Parliament from the European People's Party grouping because of its federalist tendencies, and promised that under his premiership no further transfer of power from Westminster to Brussels would take place without a referendum – a pledge which became law in the 2011 European Union Act. In government, he rejected proposals for EU-wide fiscal union, becoming the first British Prime Minister ever to veto a proposed European Treaty.

Cameron, then, certainly had a view on Europe; he just didn't think it mattered as much as other things mattered, or as much as some of his colleagues thought it did. In other words, he felt the same way about the EU as the voters. In recent history, Britain's relationship with Europe has been one of those questions on which a relatively small number of people feel very strongly indeed. They also tend to assume that others must think the same way.

Similarly, a number of MPs, most of them Conservatives, quite honourably and sincerely believed that Britain's relationship with Europe was the pre-eminent political question of our time. Some of them claimed their devotion to European questions reflected their constituents' wishes; whether they really believed this, or just pretended to, is a debatable point. What is unarguable is that, for most people, the issue has always come rather a long way down their list of priorities. (Europe)

Ipsos MORI's Issues Index contains more than forty years of monthly data showing people's answers when asked, 'What are the most important issues facing the country?' Respondents are not prompted with possible answers, and can name as many as they like. For most of the 1980s, the percentage mentioning Europe stayed in the low single figures, and climbed only as high as 18 per cent in late 1990 as Britain entered the European Exchange Rate Mechanism. In November 1991, as debate raged over the proposed new treaty ahead of the Maastricht summit, just under one third mentioned the subject, leaving it still well behind unemployment and the NHS in the priority list. The proportion reached only 22 per cent in September 1992 amid the financial turmoil that saw sterling leave the ERM. At the height of the July 1993 Maastricht rebellion, culminating in a confidence motion which could have precipitated a general election, just 19 per cent of voters named the subject that was so exercising their elected representatives (the same proportion, incidentally, that mentioned education; a quarter mentioned crime, one third mentioned the economy and the NHS, and two thirds mentioned unemployment).

In the later 1990s, Europe rose higher up the public agenda alongside the question of whether Tony Blair would try to take

XVIII • WELL, YOU DID ASK

Britain into the euro: more than two fifths named the subject during the election campaign of April 1997. The numbers drifted steadily down to just 14 per cent at the 2001 election, when one third mentioned education and two fifths the NHS (helping to explain the failure of the Tories' Europe-dominated campaign), and hardly registered thereafter except for mini-peaks spurred by specific events: 26 per cent in June 2003 on the news of the accession of ten new member states, and 19 per cent on the French and Dutch rejection of the proposed new constitution in June 2005 (the figure fell by half the following month and remained in single figures for the next nine years).

In the summer that followed Cameron's arrival in Downing Street, the proportion of voters naming Europe as a priority fell as low as 1 per cent. At the time of the backbench referendum bill, introduced to give the people the say for which they supposedly clamoured, just four in a hundred people told Ipsos MORI that Europe was one of the issues that mattered most.

The announcement of an in–out referendum, then, marked the victory of a relentless campaign, but not a popular crusade. Indeed, in January 2013, shortly after Cameron's historic speech, only a bare majority – 58 per cent – told YouGov they supported the plan. While fewer than a quarter were opposed, nearly a fifth said they didn't know whether they wanted a referendum or not.

If the voters were ambivalent towards the promised plebiscite, this was not just because of the lowly position they thought it occupied on the country's to-do list. Many also found the subject dull, confusing and wearyingly complicated.

Early in 2014, Lord Ashcroft Polls conducted a major piece of research entitled *Europe on Trial*,[1] which comprised a

---

1. *Europe on Trial*, Lord Ashcroft Polls, March 2014.

20,000-sample poll and a day-long discussion event involving eighty members of the public. This uncovered plenty of complaints. People associated the EU with excessive immigration, pointless rules and regulations, and having to pay for other countries' economic problems. Many thought that other member states seemed to get more out of the EU than Britain did. There were upsides too: free trade, unrestricted travel and, at least in theory, better relations between European countries and the comfort of being part of a team – not an insignificant point, with Russia making its presence felt on the union's borders.

But on some of the most contentious points in the European debate, people were uncertain. Did being in the EU help Britain's trade with countries outside Europe by letting us negotiate as part of a bloc, or hinder it by preventing us from hammering out free-trade deals of our own? And, if we left, would we be able to do as much trade with Europe as we do now (since the French would still want to sell us their wine and the Germans their BMWs), or would we suffer from being out of the club? Britain was divided on these things, and large numbers did not know what to think. Though two thirds thought what happened in the European Parliament had an impact on life in Britain, three quarters said they had little or no idea what went on there.

The fervent Eurosceptics thought the EU appealed most to a remote and privileged few, while many of its advocates thought their opponents narrow-minded and jingoistic. For the majority who regarded European questions with a combination of doubt and indifference, those who were ardently committed to one side or the other seemed a bit odd. As one of the participants put it, "I don't want to be the sort of person who has views about Europe."

But before long, the country was going to have to decide on one.

I. THE STARTING POINT

*"The main thing was for David Cameron to shut
his Eurosceptics up. He didn't really want a referendum."*
Focus group participant, Leeds, November 2015

By the end of 2015, it was only in the chronological sense that the country was any closer to making up its mind. In May, the Conservatives had been re-elected with an unexpected overall majority, and on 10 November, David Cameron had written to Donald Tusk, President of the European Council, setting out the reforms he sought and formally opening the process of negotiating a new deal for Britain in the EU. Most polls showed very narrow margins between the remain and leave camps.

If opinion was divided, it was not quite polarised. Research[2] by Lord Ashcroft Polls asked twenty thousand respondents to place themselves on a scale between zero, meaning they would definitely vote to stay in the EU, and one hundred, meaning they would definitely vote to leave. Overall, just under four in ten (38 per cent) put themselves in the "remain" half of the scale, between zero and forty-nine, and nearly half (47 per cent) gave themselves a score of fifty-one or above.

2. *Leave to Remain: Public Opinion and the EU Referendum* (Lord Ashcroft Polls, December 2015).

But only two fifths of the population put themselves at one end of the scale or the other, between zero and nine (firm remainers) or between ninety-one and a hundred (determined leavers); 14 per cent put themselves at exactly fifty. On both halves of the scale, a quarter of voters said they did not have a strong view and could easily be persuaded to change their minds.

Not only were many people unsure what to do, they could not see how they were going to be able to decide. Indeed, few had any clear idea of why the referendum was being held, and some rather resented having it thrust upon them. In our focus groups, those who did have an explanation nearly always said Cameron's promise had been a response to tensions among Conservative MPs, or an attempt to stop Tory voters switching to UKIP: "The main thing was for David Cameron to shut his Eurosceptics up. He didn't really want a referendum. It was because his party was split down the middle." Still, as the referendum loomed, they started to feel a weight of responsibility for making a judgement whose consequences would last a generation or more. The fact that they had not been clamouring for a referendum did not mean they thought its outcome would not matter.

For many, the decision seemed both more important and more complicated than the business of choosing a government. As one participant put it: "In a general election, if you vote one way or another it's only a few more years and you can change your vote. If we vote to come out and it happens and it's not a good thing, that's tough, you're out. They won't let us back in if we make a mistake."

The decision was all the more daunting because it was unclear what the consequences of each outcome would be, and many did not feel qualified or equipped to judge such a momentous and complicated matter. "People don't understand," one of our participants said. "I'm not being disrespectful, because I don't either." (Some were more worried about other people being let loose on the question: "I'm a *Daily Mail* reader but I'm worried about what all the other *Daily Mail* readers will do. They will read things and say, 'Well, if it's in the *Daily Mail* it must be true.'")

People wanted to know...

"What do we get for our £55 million? We can't be shelling out all that money and getting zip back, but I want to know what it is."

Accordingly, they wanted "facts". Surely, people implored, there should be an independent commission to provide the public with solid, impartial information to help them make sense of the debate? They did not expect any help on this front from the media, whose coverage would inevitably favour one side or the other. One fact that had found its way to many of the participants – a remarkable feat for a political statistic – was that Britain paid £55 million a day to be a member of the EU. Yet this, predictably enough, simply raised more questions. "What do we get for our £55 million?" someone in our groups asked. "We can't be shelling out all that money and getting zip back, but I want to know what it is."

Participants debated what they thought Britain might be getting in return. Did our trade with the EU not amount to more than that? Yes, but wouldn't they do just as much trade with us if we left? But wouldn't that be a big risk to take, and by being a member, didn't we at least get to help set the rules? But only as one of twenty-eight, so we hardly ever got our own way – and if we left could we not do our own trade deals with the rest of the world, and have more control over our borders? But wouldn't it be safer to be part of a bigger group working together?

Facts, then, would not suffice. What people really wanted were answers to questions which would always be disputed because the answers were not only unknown but unknowable: "Would we be safer as a nation? Better off? How is the economy going to work? Would we be working for less if we came out? Is our kids' future safe?" They wanted to be told what the future held inside and outside the EU, but had to conclude that nobody was going to be able to tell them: "I don't think even the politicians and economists know what the difference would be between staying and leaving. It's just guesswork."

This meant that the decision would come down to the balance of risk. The hazards inherent in leaving were the most obvious: no country had left the EU before, so however confident the Brexiteers' claims, it was impossible to be sure what the consequences of exit would be for trade, security, the economy, immigration, or for Britain's international relationships in Europe and the wider world.

Despite this, our research found only a small majority thinking a vote to leave would be the riskier option.

As our focus groups showed, people were also conscious that there were risks to remaining: given what had changed since Britain signed up to the Common Market, where was the EU heading? As more countries joined, would that mean further dilution of Britain's influence, not to mention more unrestricted immigration? Would we be compelled to help bail out failing economies, or face pressure to join the euro, or to go along with other schemes hitherto undreamt of? Remaining would mean signing up not just to the status quo, but to whatever the EU turned into.

How people saw the relative risks was determined less by "facts" than by their own preoccupations, and their own outlook on politics. The related questions of immigration into

Britain, migration into Europe from further afield, border control and national security were at the forefront of many people's minds, especially since the terrorist attacks in Paris on 13 November 2015. Some felt Britain would be safer outside the EU, believing the country would have better control of its borders, and over who was allowed to come and live here. But most did not think it would be as straightforward as this. Many felt there was "safety in numbers", and that the kind of co-operation needed to counter the security threat would happen more smoothly within the EU.

As for the volume of immigration, some argued that the UK would have more control outside the EU, sometimes because they were under the misapprehension that Britain had been set a compulsory quota for the number of migrants it was obliged to take from among those arriving in southern Europe. The fact that non-EU countries like Switzerland and Australia (the perennial exemplar of common sense in these matters) exercised stricter control over who was allowed to take up residence also carried weight.

At the same time, many did not think net immigration would actually fall if Britain were to leave the EU. There was no guarantee that a British government, left to its own devices, would be any tougher on European immigration than it was now and, in any case, people would continue to come from other parts of the world. Rather than blaming EU rules, many people put recent levels of immigration down to the idea that successive governments had been a "soft touch", especially when it came to benefits. The idea that Brexit would mean much less immigration sounded like the kind of political promise that is never quite delivered in practice. The results of our poll reflected this ambivalence. While just under four in ten agreed with the statement *We'll never be able to bring immigration under control unless we leave the EU*, almost as many thought *We won't be able to bring immigration under control* even if *we leave the EU*.

The poll gave further clues as to the voters' other competing priorities. Those inclined to leave most often mentioned immigration, border control, refugees and the UK's contribution to the EU budget among the most important things in question; for those leaning towards remaining, the biggest concerns were trade, free movement and economic security.

Asked what they thought could be at stake in the referendum, our focus group participants (none of whom had decided how to vote) came up with more than forty disparate points including trade, sovereignty, human rights, migration, national security, red tape, free movement, workers' rights, our contribution to the EU budget, and "that blue card you take on holiday in case you have to go to hospital".

The research then explored why people thought these things were important and how they thought each one affected them personally, such as effects on prices, wages, taxes, job security, safety, stability, living standards, sovereignty and international relations. We ultimately identified five overarching principles and priorities that would guide people's decisions: Security, Freedom, Independence, Belonging, and wanting to do the right thing For Future Generations.

The voters, then, were not a blank slate, or dispassionate arbiters ready to judge on the basis of dry evidence. The hopes, fears, prejudices, priorities and general view of the world with which they approached the referendum campaign would clearly be as important in their decision as what they took from it. Their task in the referendum would not be to separate the true from the false, but to decide what mattered and what did not. Rather than the facts shaping people's attitudes, the reverse would be the case: to paraphrase Paul Simon, an EU referendum voter hears what he wants to hear and disregards the rest. The job of the respective campaigns, then, would be to show that the outcome they recommended offered the best route to security, or independence, or freedom, or a sense of belonging, or the brightest legacy for people's children and grandchildren.

*

Our research began on the day of the Cameron–Tusk letter outlining the changes that would supposedly "address the concerns of the British people over our membership of the European Union". These included safeguards for non-Eurozone countries, such as ensuring that their taxpayers could never be financially liable for operations to support the euro, and that Eurozone countries could not impose decisions on member states which retained their own currencies; cutting regulations on business and extending the single market; a declaration that Britain was exempt from the drive towards "ever closer union"; more powers for national parliaments to block unwanted European legislation; and moves to end the abuse of free movement, with EU migrants having to live and pay tax in Britain for four years before claiming in-work benefits or social housing, plus an end to the practice of sending child benefit overseas.

The contents of the letter sparked a huge row in Westminster. Many Conservatives argued that the demands were much too modest, particularly when it came to tackling the level of immigration from EU countries. But while most of our participants were vaguely aware of the renegotiation that was underway, very few had any idea what was being discussed. A handful had picked up on the idea that Cameron's demands had been watered down since his earlier rhetoric on the subject. When prompted, some remembered (and strongly approved of) the four-year benefit ban for EU migrants, but nobody expected fundamental changes in Britain's relationship with Brussels, or on the things that worried them most; at best, there might be small improvements at the margins. As one participant observed: "I don't think things like immigration are going to be up for discussion. It will be maybe 0.5 per cent of this or that." There was also the problem that "people don't know what the current deal is. So I wouldn't know if the new one was any better."

Fewer than one in five people, including only just over one third of Conservative voters, said they had much confidence that Cameron would be able to win a better deal in his talks with fellow European leaders. But, at the same time, more than one in three said they would be more likely to vote for Britain to stay in the EU if the Prime Minister recommended it on the basis of the new terms he had secured. Crucially, half of those who had voted Conservative at the general election said this, even though a majority of Tories had put themselves on the "leave" side of our 100-point scale and saw staying in the EU as a bigger risk than leaving. Though they were pessimistic about Cameron's chances of achieving much in the renegoti-ation, they looked by far the most likely to respond if he was able to claim victory convincingly. As another participant said of the splendid new deal that would doubtless be announced when talks were over: "I don't think I'd believe it, to be honest. Who's going to police it?" Trust in Cameron personally, and particularly his ability to persuade his own voters, would be critical to the outcome.

However, the electorate did not divide along neat party lines: differences in people's underlying attitudes were much more telling. Those leaning towards voting to leave were much more likely than remainers to think that life in Britain was worse today than it was thirty years ago; that for most children growing up in Britain today, life would be worse than it was for their parents; that the way the economy was changing brought more threats than opportunities to their standard of living; that immigration had been a bad thing for the country; and that recent changes in society had been mostly for the worse. They were also less likely to think that feminism, globalisation, the green movement, multiculturalism and social liberalism had been forces for good.

But neither did the electorate divide tidily between leavers, remainers and doubters. In fact, analysis of our 20,000-sample poll identified seven distinct segments of voters, according to their combinations of views.

Nothing to Lose voters, who made up nearly a quarter of the population, leaned heavily towards leaving. Many were retired, or not working. They overwhelmingly thought immigration had been bad for Britain, and tended to be pessimistic both for themselves and for the country. They were much more likely than most to have voted UKIP at the general election, and were unlikely to be swayed by Cameron's view. They thought Britain was a worse place to live than it was thirty years ago, and took a dim view of multiculturalism, social liberalism, feminism and the green movement. They thought the main questions at stake in the referendum were immigration and border control, which they saw largely in terms of pressure on public services, jobs, wages and entitlement to benefits.

One in eight voters was in the *Global Britain* segment. They also favoured Brexit, but were different in background and attitude from the *Nothing to Lose* group, tending to be younger, professional and the most likely of any segment to

be from an Asian background. They were optimistic for themselves and the country, happy with the way life had turned
out for them, and saw more opportunities than threats in the
changing economy. They also had a more positive view than
most of globalisation, multiculturalism, immigration and
(especially) capitalism.

3/ *Hard-Pressed Undecideds*, who made up nearly a fifth of the
electorate, had largely backed Labour over the Tories at the election. They saw immigration and border control as the biggest
issues at stake in the referendum, especially in terms of their
effect on prices and economic stability, but doubted that these
problems would be solved by leaving. Nevertheless, they tended
to think that remaining was the risker option. They felt under
pressure from changes in society and the economy, and were
more likely than most to say the country was on the wrong
track and that it matters little who wins elections because
nothing changes for people like them.

4/ The *Listen to DC* group, which made up another eighth of
the population, were a crucial group as far as the renegotiation
was concerned. Though undecided, they saw leaving the EU as
a bigger risk than staying and were the most likely to say David
Cameron could persuade them to vote to remain. When it
came to issues at stake in the referendum, they were, unusually,
almost as likely to mention free movement and free trade as immigration and border control, and their higher-level concerns
were economic stability, living standards, security and future
generations. More generally, they were optimistic, believing
it is possible for someone who works hard to be successful in
Britain whatever their background, and that recent changes
in society had on the whole been for the better. They were
more likely than most to think multiculturalism, globalisation
and immigration had been forces for good.

5 The slightly smaller *If It Ain't Broke* group leaned heavily towards staying, seeing leaving the EU as the riskier option by a wide margin. Their biggest concerns were trade, free movement and economic security, and they were the most likely of all to say we would not be able to control immigration even if we leave the EU. Members were divided over whether Britain was on the right track, and more likely than most to think it matters little who wins elections.

6 *I'm Alright, Jacques* voters, comprising just over a tenth of the population, wanted to stay. They tended to be affluent, to work in the private sector, to be engaged in current affairs, and were more likely than most to support the Conservatives. They saw leaving as a risk, saw the debate in terms of economic security and trade, and did not see Brexit as an effective way to control immigration. They were optimistic, and much more positive than most about multiculturalism, globalisation, capitalism and immigration.

7 Just under one voter in ten was in a segment we called *Citizens of the World*. These were the keenest of all to remain. They tended to be younger, with a higher than average number of students, recent graduates and professionals. They thought free movement, human rights, free trade and economic security were the issues at stake in the referendum; few mentioned immigration. They valued having fundamental rights guaranteed by Europe, and thought Britain benefited from strength in numbers and co-operation within the EU. Of all the segments, the *Citizens of the World* had the most positive view of immigration, multiculturalism, social liberalism, feminism and the green movement, but the most negative view of capitalism. They were also more likely than most to think that people from some backgrounds would never have a real chance to succeed no matter how hard they worked.

So, although many voters felt lost in the face of the decision before them, their view of the world, and of what matters, predisposed them to vote one way or the other. But that is not to say the campaigns would make no difference. People's background views were, after all, firmer and more enduring than their opinion, if they had one, on whether or not Britain should be a member of the EU. The associations people made with each option would also have an important part to play. Though they were uncertain on a number of fronts, most of our participants said a decision to leave the EU would feel more like a step backwards than a step forward. Though some argued that leaving would show confidence and independence, the more prevalent view was that Brexit would be a move towards isolation and away from the modern world – and, for a few, a vote against foreigners, European cultural influences, co-operation and the future.

For some, this view was reinforced by the individuals and parties on each side of the debate, and the kinds of voters who would follow them. As one focus group participant put it: "David Cameron and Nicola Sturgeon and Ed Miliband and probably Jeremy Corbyn are in favour of staying. The people who want out are UKIP, the extreme right wing. I don't know enough about the arguments but it's about whom you trust." Asked in our poll whether certain adjectives applied more to one campaign or the other, majorities thought the remain side sounded more "moderate", "normal", "reasonable" and "sensible"; only two – "patriotic" and "fanatical" – were decisively associated with those campaigning to leave.

Ultimately, the task for the leave and remain camps was to show that their side represented the best means to the ends people wanted. Was our physical and economic security better served through independence from Europe or as part of a wider union?

Did they want freedom from interference in the making of our laws, or the freedom to work and travel throughout the EU with rights guaranteed whichever party ruled in Westminster? If they valued the sense of belonging, was it to belong to an exceptional island nation or to a broader civilisation of diverse cultures but shared values? If they voted to leave, would the future generations for whom they were anxious to do the right thing find themselves isolated or liberated?

In the political world, these arguments had already been going on for generations, or felt as though they had. For many voters, they were only just beginning.

APPENDIX TO CHAPTER I

The 20,000-sample December 2015 poll that was the basis for our Leave To Remain *project included a "laddering" exercise, in which people identified the issues that mattered to them most, what they thought the impact would be on themselves and their families, and then the higher-level consequences, values and principles that were at stake. Here we see the thought processes for the most determined leave and remain voters ("Nothing to Lose" and "Citizens of the World"), and the two least committed to one side or the other ("Hard-Pressed Undecideds" and "Listen to DC"), six months before the referendum.*

"Nothing to Lose"

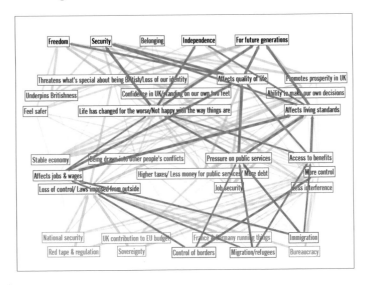

"Citizens of the World"

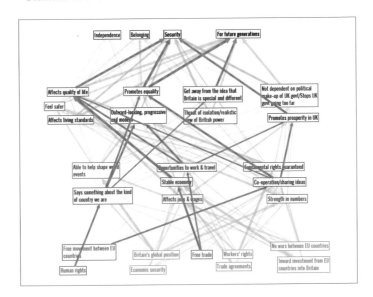

"Hard-Pressed Undecideds"

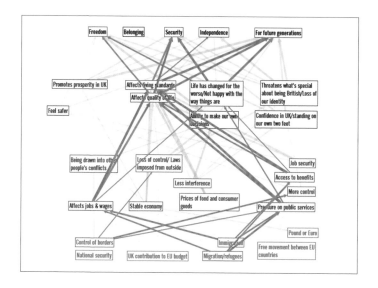

"Listen to DC"

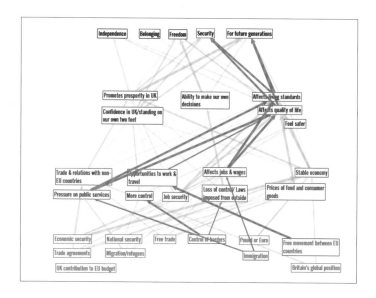

II. JEUX SANS FRONTIÈRES

"The British just do their own thing.
They're like Switzerland, but an island."
<small>Focus group participant, Amsterdam, February 2016</small>

The Prime Minister's plan to keep his country in the EU depended on offering voters something other than the status quo: instead, they would have the chance to choose a new deal for Britain in a reformed union. Achieving such a deal would mean exercising his persuasive power on his fellow European leaders, whose people had their own views, often rather trenchant, about their place in Europe – and about Britain.

Although Britain had often seemed to its neighbours to be only a reluctant player on the European stage, we found in our research[3] in the run-up to the renegotiation that British voters were by no means the least enthusiastic members of the EU. That distinction went to the Czechs, who, when asked to rate how positive they felt about their membership on a scale from zero to one hundred, gave a score of forty-five. Next came the Swedes, with fifty-one. This put the UK, with fifty-two, as the joint third least avid member, alongside Denmark and Austria.

3. *You Should Hear What They Say About You*, Lord Ashcroft Polls, February 2016. Online poll of 28,720 adults in all twenty-eight EU countries.

At the time of the renegotiation

The Dutch managed to muster one extra notch of ardour, with fifty-three. At the other end of the scale, the keenest of all were the Maltese, who awarded a score of seventy-six, followed by Spain, Poland, Ireland and Lithuania.

Among Britain's twenty-seven fellow members, the single most important benefit of the EU was *being able to travel freely throughout other EU countries* (though, in the UK, this was trumped by *free trade with other EU countries*). This was particularly the case for "New Europe", the countries which had joined in 2004 or later, where three quarters of respondents chose free travel as one of the biggest advantages. Seven in ten also chose *being able to live and work in other EU countries*, compared to just under half in "Old Europe" (while people in Britain named *the scale of immigration from other EU countries* as the biggest single downside of membership).

For the latest accession states, as we found in focus groups around the continent, the ability to travel and work abroad represented more than just a chance to earn more than they could at home, important though that was. As one Bulgarian participant explained in the first of our focus groups involving people from a range of backgrounds in EU capital cities, "The opportunity to work abroad is the most important part. It saves thousands of families, especially north of Sofia. Bulgaria is probably sustained by the money people send from abroad – if we were not part of the EU it would be hell on earth here." But in former communist countries where free travel was a relative novelty, the sense of liberty they felt was valuable in itself. The important point, as a man in Warsaw said, is that "overnight you can decide you want to go somewhere. You can just go, take a look at the labour market and make a decision." A lady in Latvia, old enough to remember life as part of the USSR, underlined the principle: "I don't want to live anywhere else, but I need to have the feeling that if I want to, I can go."

"Overnight you can decide you want to go somewhere. You can just go, take a look at the labour market and make a decision."

If unrestricted travel represented prosperity, opportunity and freedom for individuals, for their countries there was another side to the coin: "Bulgaria is losing its experts. Everyone goes abroad, especially doctors. We're losing our brains." Younger people would not choose to make their future at home, so "when the elderly die we will be lost as a nation. Only the gypsies will remain." Warsaw participants complained that "we are paying taxes to pay for universities in Poland for people to train as doctors and go abroad" and that "in twenty years we won't have anything to pay pensions from".

In our poll, around half of Croatians, Latvians and Lithuanians, two fifths of Bulgarians and more than a quarter of Poles said *too many people going to live and work abroad* was one of the biggest downsides of EU membership. Not that our focus groups blamed anyone who made such a choice: "It's because they're in a small town with no job, not because they wanted to. If you're working in a clothes shop you can't support yourself, even the rent. If the rent is 1,000 zloty and you earn 1,400, what can you do?"; "Young people are leaving because there are no prospects here and you can earn more money washing dishes there." Our Bulgarians were the most pessimistic of all: "Anyone who has gone abroad has saved themselves."

Throughout Europe, the question of free movement now had other troubling implications. More than a million asylum seekers had arrived in Germany in 2015; Berlin's old Tempelhof

Airport, converted to become a popular public space in 2010, had become home to seven thousand refugees, with temporary buildings and facilities including a school and kindergarten. A riot had erupted at the site in the weeks before our visit, and in Cologne on New Year's Eve, hundreds of women were assaulted by men reported to be of Arab and North African origin.

"I don't think they will integrate … when there is
a barbecue party at school and 30 per cent of
the kids are Syrians, will there still be pork sausages?"

Even in Germany's liberal capital, the situation was a source of tension. Though most in our groups still thought migration was beneficial overall ("We need someone to pay for our retirement!"), several said they or their partners felt less safe in the streets. For many, the sheer number of arrivals made successful integration impossible, threatening the country's generally good community relations. Some feared they would be expected to adapt to the incomers, rather than the other way round: "I don't think they will integrate – we will adapt to meet their needs. When there is a barbecue party at school and 30 per cent of the kids are Syrians, will there still be pork sausages?"

In Sweden, which had taken more asylum seekers relative to its population than any other country in Europe, the question of migrants was "the only thing people talk about. It's becoming us against them." Our participants thought their government had been well-intentioned but ill-prepared: "I am for helping people as much as possible but I don't think we have been wise … There was no thinking of the consequences."

"The numbers that should have been divided between
twenty-eight countries went to three countries:

*Germany, Sweden and Denmark. There is supposed
to be solidarity in the EU, but there is no solidarity."*

In both Germany and Sweden, much of the resentment was aimed at their European neighbours, who seemed to have abandoned the principle of free movement and the idea of co-operating to solve common problems. "Our mistake was expecting the EU to be there to help," one Swede told us. "The numbers that should have been divided between twenty-eight countries went to three countries: Germany, Sweden and Denmark. There is supposed to be solidarity in the EU, but there is no solidarity." This did not bode well, people thought. "Schengen will die. People are building walls." Some in Berlin suspected that what they called "our difficult history" was one reason their government had felt unable to take a tougher line on the migrant crisis: "We and our children are paying for our past again."

The situation was felt perhaps most acutely of all in Greece, where more than forty thousand migrants were unable to move on as neighbouring states closed their borders. The Prime Minister, Alexis Tsipras, had recently warned that his country was in danger of becoming "a warehouse of souls". Again, there was no malice towards those who had arrived on their shores – "people are running for their lives". But, as for the EU, "It's not a union, is it? We're supposed to be a member of the European family." Instead, "they have abandoned us to the mercy of heaven".

Playing by the rules

If, for Britain's fellow members, the biggest advantage of the

EU was the extension of liberty offered by free movement, the biggest downside was the idea of being told what to do, or *the imposition of unnecessary rules and regulations.* Half of all participants named this as a disadvantage in our poll, with higher numbers recorded in non-Eurozone, smaller and newer member states (including three quarters in Estonia and the Czech Republic).

Throughout Europe, the groups had plenty of examples to complain about: rules about household waste, smoking, toll roads, health and safety, agricultural and fishing quotas, nuclear power generation, VAT, building inspections, preservation of peat bogs and the production of traditional cheese – not to mention the dimensions of cucumbers and bananas – were all spontaneously mentioned as examples of EU interference. Rather than trying to resist this tendency, national governments would often make things worse – a complaint often heard in Britain but echoed elsewhere (though some participants in Germany and Sweden made the opposite complaint, that Europe-wide rules had diluted their own standards). A man in Warsaw told of his experience of trying to open a bar: "Every time they came to inspect, something was wrong. Everything was fine but they said I had to raise the ceiling seven centimetres. I already had debts. I thought, 'I'm going to jump in the river.' So I looked it up, and it turned out it wasn't a regulation, it was a recommendation. If anyone says there is an EU regulation, ask them to show it to you."

> *"The French eat snails but they categorise them as fish so they can get subsidies."*

More annoying than the rules themselves was the suspicion that nobody else was sticking to them – or, at least, that those who broke them did so with impunity. The main culprits were thought to be the southern European countries and, by common consent, the French, who manipulated or ignored directives as they saw fit: "The French eat snails but they categorise them as fish so they can get subsidies"; "France didn't meet the budget deficit rule but there was no cost. But we always hand in our homework on time," complained a man in Amsterdam. "It's like a classroom, you need rules. But the richest boys in the class, who know the teacher, can pass with a lower grade, and the poorer ones with the criminal parents get let off." The Dutch were "the best behaved boys in the class", not that it did them any good.

The worst offenders of all, however, were the Greeks, whose apparent attitude to authority inspired a mix of exasperation and wonder. "The Commission flew over to check the olive fields and they put up artificial trees!" marvelled a man in Riga. "They introduced a pool tax, and everyone put these green rollers over their pool so they couldn't be spotted," a man in Dublin recalled. "Though, to be honest, that sounds like quite an Irish thing to do." This disdain for the rules was also, for many, at the root of the country's currency crisis: "I don't know who accepted them to be in the Eurozone," a French participant said. "We knew the figures were tampered with." (Though that was not to say there should be no bailouts: "It might be our turn next!")

"We just need to tell the Greeks to start working. They're not paying taxes but we're supposed to pay them?"

But as far as our groups were concerned, Greece's predicament was not just a matter of the currency. The view was the same everywhere. In Latvia: "How they live! People go there for their summer holidays and they don't do anything during the winter." In Bulgaria: "Their pensions are higher than our salaries!" In Poland: "They created the mess for themselves. We just need to tell the Greeks to start working. They're not paying taxes but we're supposed to pay them? What for?" In Ireland: "They don't produce anything, they import everything, even olives." Ireland had also had to turn to Europe for help after its own crisis. Was there any difference between the two situations? "Yes! We're paying it back! They just don't believe in paying tax. We always pay our way."

Not surprisingly, given these views, *having to pay for other countries' economic problems* was rated the second biggest downside of EU membership in our Europe-wide poll: more than half of those in northern EU countries said this was an important disadvantage (though less than two fifths in southern countries did so).

This, incidentally, explains why the feeling in the focus groups was heavily against admitting new members to the EU. Albania, Macedonia, Montenegro, Serbia and Turkey were all candidate countries, and none sounded like very good prospects to most of our participants. "They're all quite poor," observed a participant in Germany, "so we'll have to pay for them as well." With the recent expansion and the refugee crisis, "we have enough problems as it is. We shouldn't accept more dependents in the family." Similarly, in Dublin: "I'd doubt the political stability of all those countries. Albania is probably a third-world country. What the EU would have to put in would be phenomenal." For some, there was nothing wrong in principle with admitting new members, but experience made them cautious: "If I thought they'd stick to the rules after they joined, I'd agree," as a Dutch participant put it, "but I don't have that feeling." The absence of common values was another problem with further expansion. Some felt the existing members were too numerous and too diverse to constitute a coherent union: "Estonia, Latvia, Turkey – they have different cultures from the European one. It's not going to work, it's too big"; "They're too different. Who are these people? I don't know anything about them."

> *"It's easy to blame foreigners rather than ourselves …*
> *It's not the foreigners' fault there are so many public*
> *servants in this country."*

In Greece itself, meanwhile, the biggest drawbacks were seen as *loss of national sovereignty, with laws and decisions being made by people we did not elect*, chosen by three quarters of Greek participants, and *austerity imposed on my country by the EU against our will*, chosen by more than two thirds. In a referendum the previous July, Greek voters had rejected the bailout conditions proposed by the European Commission, only for their government to accept austerity measures harsher than those that had been put before the people. Despite this, our groups in Athens were notably un-defiant. If some of the measures were painful and had been accepted "at gunpoint", few held the EU responsible for the crisis: "It's easy to blame foreigners rather than ourselves … It's not the foreigners' fault there are so many public servants in this country." The truth was that Greece had "spent out-rageously" and that generous help from Europe over many years had "made us lazy. With all the subsidies, a lot of people found the easy way out, and they weren't invested as they should have been." It was no use complaining now that times had changed: "It's like having a teacher at school who pampers you and gives you the answers and then starts being strict." Greeks had made the most of low interest rates since joining the euro by borrowing lavishly, and "when it's time to pay, we blame the lenders for asking for their money". Though some blamed the politicians for allowing Greece to reach such a state, they understood if people in other countries were impatient: "It must have driven everybody crazy. Everyday people, who were paying their taxes, were saying, 'Why should we be lending to Greece, with their pensions?' What age do you think they get their pension in Germany? Sixty-five!"

Who runs the show?

At the root of the complaints about interfering rules and regulations and having to help bail out feckless neighbours was *loss of national sovereignty, with laws and decisions being made by people we did not elect.* This was the fourth biggest disadvantage of EU membership as far as British voters were concerned, and the third most important for those in the twenty-seven other countries: four in ten named it as a downside, though it was chosen more often in small countries than big, and more often outside than inside the Eurozone.

"What influence does a Bulgarian politician have? He's happy if a German politician pats him on the shoulder."

"You don't have influence as an individual country," said one of our Berlin participants, "you have to agree things as a group. That's what it's all about." That is easy for you to say, others elsewhere might have replied had they heard him. "What influence does a Bulgarian politician have?" asked one in Sofia. "He's happy if a German politician pats him on the shoulder ... My grandmother always said, 'The Germans lost the war but they're still dealing the cards.'" And in Athens: "Have you seen where Tsipras stands in the EU photographs? At the far end on the left!" Most did not feel strongly that EU membership was eroding their national identity ("People in Cyprus are not going to dance our national dance, and we're not going to dance theirs," as someone put it in Riga), but any idea that power was shared between countries equally, or anything like equally, was dismissed. "There are two EUs," observed a man in Warsaw. "EU number one was the founders, and the others joined later and are treated worse." "I think we're well liked, well respected," said a lady in Dublin, "but I don't think we have much of a say. Does our opinion really matter when the big countries can overrule whatever?" As for the Greeks: "During the negotiations they wanted to eat us!"

Three things conferred clout, people thought: size, wealth and being a longstanding part of the European establishment. In other words, Germany ran the show. In our poll, nearly three quarters of British respondents, and 84 per cent of those in the twenty-seven other countries, named Germany as one of the three countries with the most influence over EU decisions (rising to a near-unanimous 96 per cent in Greece). France was next, chosen by 58 per cent of Britons and nearly two thirds in the twenty-seven as a whole. In third place was the UK, though respondents elsewhere in Europe were nearly twice as likely as the British themselves to think the country had a big influence in the EU.

Some in our Berlin groups were bemused that people in other countries should think Germany dominated European decision-making ("Do they really? Which countries?"), and a few offered unlikely explanations ("I think it's because Martin Schulz is President of the Parliament and he is German").

Though they could see why Germany seemed to others to be in charge, that was not how it felt to them: "It probably looks like that from the outside because Angela Merkel has lots of things to say, but they are not accepted by others so what's the use?" Germany, they argued, was just as constrained as its neighbours by the pooling of sovereignty, "but otherwise it wouldn't work. You can't have a union without anything binding."

Glad you came?

For the new accession states, giving up some control over their own affairs had been an accepted part of the deal. "Of course you give up sovereignty, it's a joint venture," as a man in Latvia put it. "If you're playing with others in the sandbox, you have to pay attention to everyone." Whether the benefits that had been promised in return had ever materialised was a matter of debate.

> *"We longed for freedom, for a standard of living*
> *like the West … We associated the EU with*
> *progress, development, Germany, France,*
> *a better quality of life."*

In Bulgaria, Poland and Latvia, the three countries we visited which had acceded since 2004, most of our participants had been in favour of joining at the time. They gave similar reasons: the expectation of "European" incomes and living standards, the chance to travel and work across the continent, the promise of lavish funding for infrastructure and other projects: "We longed for freedom, for a standard of living like the West," said a man in Warsaw. "We associated the EU with progress, development, Germany, France, a better quality of life."

In Latvia in particular, people also welcomed the prospect of extra security against the threat from "our Eastern neighbour". Do Latvia's EU membership and its relations with Russia really have anything to do with each other? "Could you ask a more stupid question? … Latvia is so small, it has to be part of some union. We need to be part of something bigger because we couldn't exist on our own"; "Russia does what it wants. They attack individual countries. You can never tell what our Eastern neighbour will do." Latvians had wanted to join "so we wouldn't be outside. Otherwise Russia would take over."

The anticipated improvement in living standards had not materialised, at least not to the degree they felt had been promised. Costs had risen to European levels, but not incomes: "We always hoped that salaries would be like European salaries, but we never get there. Our expenses are, but not our salaries"; "They have unified prices, but not wages. It is forcing German prices on us but we are not earning the same as they are in Germany." In Latvia, people thought joining the euro had aggravated this problem; in Poland and Bulgaria, fear of the same thing happening was the biggest objection to abandoning the zloty and the lev.

> *"They have unified prices, but not wages.*
> *It is forcing German prices on us but we are*
> *not earning the same as they are in Germany."*

One acknowledged consequence of EU membership was the bounty of the widely advertised "Eurofunds", particularly to help upgrade infrastructure. These had been abundant ("We weren't aware we would get so much money. I didn't imagine it!") and had done some good: "The Polish state is more affluent. In the smallest villages and towns you will see renovated market-places, streets and roads." But, by and large, "it didn't get into our hands". To our groups, EU subsidies were synonymous with waste and (in Bulgaria) corruption as much as with the improvements they had brought. "We get European funds for certain things. But they are not managed as they should be and they are not transparent"; "It's good for a percentage of the population. A few have got a lot, but they were getting a lot before that"; "When the government builds two kilometres of road there is a big ceremony. Then, in three months, cracks appear in infrastructure projects, literal cracks."

While the Warsaw groups thought funds could have been better used (they complained about the building of airports which have since struggled to attract passengers), some in Sofia believed Bulgaria had become more reliant on Eurofunds because of the damage they thought other aspects of EU membership had done to the country's industry. Where they had hoped being part of a wider union would mean a bigger market for Bulgarian products, the result seemed to have been more imports and higher prices: "Agriculture is ruined – now we have to buy fruit and vegetables from abroad. How come we're importing tomatoes from Poland? We used to export tomatoes to Poland."

Despite these quibbles, there was a feeling – particularly evident in the Warsaw groups – that EU membership represented progress. "When we entered the EU we became part of the global economy," one participant observed. "We used to be a separate economy." Free movement had brought costs as well as opportunities, as discussed above, but was an important part of the way Poland had changed: "We used to have to learn languages from a textbook. Last summer I walked down the boulevards and about 40 per cent of the conversations were in English, French, German! That was unthinkable ten years ago." The country had found a new confidence: "There is no inferiority complex now. We used to think if it was invented in the West, it must be better. But I don't think young people think that any more." The neighbours had noticed, too, they thought: "The Ukrainians really admire us. And Belarus. They admire how much we've changed."

> *"There is no inferiority complex now. We used to think*
> *if it was invented in the West, it must be better.*
> *But I don't think young people think that any more."*

Our groups in Sofia took a rather more gloomy view. Not only were things no better (or even worse) than they had been outside the EU, many looked back fondly to life under communism. "According to my mother it was just great. They went on holiday twice a year, now it's once if you're lucky. It was more secure, less stressful … Ordinary people, the working class, used to live much better than they do now." Participants recalled a time when "we were carefree. There was employment for everyone. If you wanted to study you could study, if you wanted to work you could work. The money was little but there was enough for everything." (Few in our Warsaw groups had any nostalgia for the old regime: "I think we had ration cards! Forget about the old days. I was raised in that system. I wouldn't like to go back, it's incomparable. Some say it's better but they have very short memories." This was echoed in Riga: "It's completely different, it can't be compared. You can at least say what you think.")

For our Bulgarian participants, EU membership did not make them feel fully part of the club. One woman recalled: "I was in France for two months but not for a second did I feel equal to them. It was like living in a movie. They don't accept us." Some felt their status within the union was below that of other countries which had only recently acceded: "They accepted Poland, Hungary and Slovakia as brothers, but we are like savages – allowed in the backyard but not in the house." Part of the reason, they thought, was that being part of the EU's external border, Bulgaria was seen as a problem: "a transit zone for criminals and drugs".

> *"They accepted Poland, Hungary and Slovakia*
> *as brothers, but we are like savages – allowed in*
> *the backyard but not in the house."*

Other comments suggested this view owed more to a lack of confidence about how they measured up to their neighbours than to any actual snub from a fellow member: "We are lacking the standards and culture, the things we need to call ourselves European"; countries like Britain "are light years ahead of us. Even if we were running towards each other, we would never reach them." Neither did they think their leaders were doing much to improve perceptions: "When David Cameron came here, Borissov [the Bulgarian Prime Minister] told him he had been patted on the head by three popes. What can I say?"

Yet even in more confident Warsaw, people still felt there was a way to go before Poland and the Poles were considered to be on a level with the more established members. Though they were now regarded differently in some places, notably Britain, "Spain still treats us like the third world. In Germany they still joke that we steal cars. I said, 'What about those paintings you stole from us that are still hanging in German museums?'"

Land of lions (and monkeys)

This, then, was how things looked to Britain's European neighbours in early 2016: at home, uncertainty about the economy and the prospects for future generations ranging from very cautious optimism to deep pessimism; worries about the long-term effects of migration (in Warsaw, supplier of abundant migrant labour to the West, it was noted that "even in McDonald's there are recruitment ads in Polish and Ukrainian. It's a sign of the times"); doubts that public services would be able to keep pace with demand; concerns about domestic and international security; and scepticism that governments had the capacity or inclination to deal effectively with any of these things. The European Union brought benefits in terms of trade, co-operation and free movement (especially their own), but subjected them to laws made by people they did not elect, imposed tiresome rules that fellow members seemed to ignore, forced them to pay for others' profligacy, and ran its finances in a manner that was opaque if not corrupt.

In other words, on the face of it, continental voters had much the same outlook on politics as their counterparts across the English Channel. But, as we found, their attitude to Britain itself revealed that, at a deeper level, many took a different approach to the European question.

In our Europe-wide poll, people rated thirty-four countries, including all EU members, according to how positive or negative they felt towards them (the participant's own country was excluded from the list). The UK received an average favourability rating of seventy-two out of a hundred, putting it in second place in the league table behind only Sweden, with seventy-four. (When we asked our Stockholm focus groups why they thought they were so popular, they were Swedishly modest: "People think Sweden is the promised land. Parental leave, dads staying at home with the kids – people know all about this"; "It's because we're not that controversial. We're pretty timid when we go out into the world"; "It's because of the welfare system, and individuals like Olof Palme, and Nobel"; "Well, yes, and Abba. And Ikea.") More than four fifths of respondents gave the UK a positive rating of fifty-one or above, and those aged between eighteen and twenty-four gave the country a higher score than any other age group. The highest ratings came from Malta, Estonia, Romania, Denmark, Lithuania, Poland and Portugal.

In our poll, people chose from a list of twenty-five options the word or phrase that first came to mind when they thought of the UK. "Polite" came top, followed by "patriotic" and "cosmopolitan"; "status-conscious" and "arrogant" were the next most likely to be chosen. Significantly or otherwise, those living in Eurozone countries were twice as likely as others to think the UK "arrogant".

> *"They have strange hobbies, like walking out*
> *in the fog and hunting for foxes."*

We asked our focus group participants around Europe what they thought of Britain (without telling them they were being listened to by Brits and that their words would be read by a mainly British audience). Their comments revealed a generally positive mixture of admiration, respect, and cheerful bemusement towards a country of baffling eccentricities. The peculiarities were often the first things to be mentioned ("They drive on the wrong side. Even the trains are on the wrong side"; "They have more housewives than we have"; "They have that special British black humour that is impossible for us to understand"; "They have strange hobbies, like walking out in the fog and hunting for foxes"; "Snooker – an excellent sport!"), or the unfortunate afflictions Brits had to endure – particularly the weather ("Moist, fog. But nice for women's skins. That's why they don't have wrinkles") and the food ("Oh my God. Fish and chips"; "They have meat and this mint gravy. Oh, it's disgusting"; "Their breakfasts – fatty sausages and beans"; "The Germans eat pork knuckle, we eat pork knuckle. The English eat lamb. What kind of meat is that?"). Bad diet had its inevitable consequence: "They think we're all very thin [in France], but we live healthily and eat well. We're not Americanised like them, so we're not obese."

> *"The English eat lamb. What kind of meat is that?"*

For some, especially in Greece and the accession states, Britain represented order and steadiness, compared to what they felt they were used to: "It's a very well-arranged, tidy country"; "They have political stability … They might be cold people but the country is dynamic and advanced"; "In Latvia we have three political parties for every two people, so there is more order there." Commitment to tradition gave rise to anachronisms, however: "How they vote [in Parliament] – 'ayeee'. It's like a hundred years ago."

> *"It's a multicultural society. You can have any job you want as a woman with a headscarf."*

Throughout Europe, our participants spontaneously said Britain seemed commendably open and welcoming, in contrast to other European countries: "London is very cosmopolitan. There is no discrimination as there is in France, for example.

They are more open to other nations"; "It's a multicultural society. You can have any job you want as a woman with a headscarf"; "The Germans don't trust foreigners so easily. Brits are more open." For some, though, this rarely went beyond tolerance to a more personal interest: "Immigrants are a specific caste. No Brit will invite an immigrant home for dinner. Maybe by the second or third generation you will be allowed to be a real friend with a Brit."

This, however, would probably owe more to the famous British reserve than any unfriendliness or desire to exclude. "They're not so emotional. They love formality. They're very conservative"; "Cold. We're warmer, more temperamental, emotional. English people can't have fun as we do." In Germany, this exchange took place: "They think we're stiff." "They think *we're* stiff? That's funny."

Although there was "a certain correctness", those who had been to the UK or had dealings with British people often said how friendly they found them: "If you take out a map, people approach and try to help"; "The queueing is very nice. There is a nice atmosphere on the subway. They are very polite"; "They're always happy and open and even if things are not OK they will smile and say, 'How are you?'"; "They're more friendly than other people, especially considering my English." A lady in Dublin had been in England during the Italia '90 World Cup: "I was an embarrassment but people were very tolerant. I couldn't believe how nice they were."

> *"They're drunk as hell. They're always getting kicked out of hotels."*

Overall, "a noble people, decent", "elegant, phlegmatic", though "a bit culturally odd, sometimes". One such idiosyncrasy was that "they are very polite but they freak out and go crazy like hooligans"; "They don't go out and party, they go out drinking. They say, 'Let's go out drinking.' They get wasted." This trait had been noticed particularly in the Netherlands ("They're drunk as hell. They're always getting kicked out of hotels"), Latvia ("English tourists who come here have a strange hobby of peeing on the Freedom Monument. But where can you find a toilet at five a.m. in Riga?"), Greece (where, in our poll, "binge drinkers" was the second most chosen phrase when asked what came to mind when they thought of the UK), and Spain: "In Ibiza and Majorca, you can tell who's British from a distance. The families are great but the young people are savages." In particular, "the young women are looking for what they're looking for, if you know what I mean. The little skanks."

> "I feel sorry for British people. They work to the bone. There are people going to the gym at a quarter to six in the morning."

A few took a dim view of the British work ethic, suggesting that this explained the need for so many European workers: "A Latvian will do two people's jobs. Brits will be very slow, and drink their tea." More often, they saw the UK as a more dynamic and entrepreneurial country than most of the continent, with a more American-style attitude to work and business. Not that they always saw this as something to emulate or aspire to: "They have a more deregulated system, like the US. They have a weaker social state than we have"; "I feel sorry for British people. They work to the bone. There are people going to the gym at a quarter to six in the morning"; "I admire the UK because of what they've achieved but I wouldn't want to live like them."

For similar reasons, "the gap between rich and poor is

very big. If you have a lot of money you go to a private school, if not you go on social security"; "We have more equality [in the Netherlands], in the sense of richer and poorer. If you're on a tram, we don't say, 'This part is for the rich'"; "You hear a lot about the class system, which we don't really have here [in Germany]."

> *"At Yalta, with the USA they passed us over to Stalin.*
> *So thanks to them, the Poles ended up in the East. And after*
> *303 Squadron fought with them in the Battle of Britain!"*

Predictably, history played a big part in perceptions of Britain and, according to our participants, in explaining why the country and its people were as they were. This was especially so for those who took a less favourable view. Being "a small island that has conquered all those countries", which had once had "colonies and governors", the UK was prone to arrogance, and to looking down on its neighbours. If two world wars continued to shade how some in Britain saw their continental neighbours, the reverse was also true. "I think of the attitude they have had to us in the past," said a lady in Bulgaria. "The bombardment of Sofia in World War Two ... They have never been our friends. Even though Borissov thinks he's friends with David Cameron, which is funny." And in Greece: "I think of Cyprus. We don't have good memories." And in Ireland: "Britain's history with so many countries is military. I don't think they get that. There is huge resentment towards them throughout the world because of that ... They're a bit gung-ho, like the Yanks." And even in Poland: "At Yalta, with the USA they passed us over to Stalin. So thanks to them, the Poles ended up in the East. And after 303 Squadron fought with them in the Battle of Britain!"

If the UK were an animal, we asked each of our groups,

what kind of animal would it be? As is often the case with this kind of research, this apparently superficial question revealed some quite nuanced views. In nearly every group someone said they thought of Britain as a lion: "For centuries they ruled the world. It's not like that any more but they still have huge influence"; "Because of the kingdom. And the lion has a big mouth"; "They want to be in charge"; "They like to be the leader of the pack"; "The head of a lion and the bottom of a bear." Less charitably, "economically, it could be an eagle, but politically it is an old lion just before it dies. Or in a zoo, sterilised. It thinks it has an empire but on the global map it plays no role at all."

> *"They are cut off from Europe.*
> *They are living there on that island."*

There were plenty of other suggestions. A horse, because "Britain is not as powerful as it is classy. A very excellent, good breed of horse with a pedigree"; an elephant, because "an elephant is a slow, heavy, conservative animal. It's smart and it does a lot of work" and because it is "strong and powerful but not aggressive"; a dog, because "it is honest but can also bite" and "knows what to do and when to do it. Really well trained. If it smells something, off it goes," or more specifically a bulldog, because "a bulldog is calm but you wouldn't want to piss it off"; a monkey, because "they don't let themselves be ruled by anyone", "it sits on your shoulder looking at the situation, and if it thinks something is being taken away from it, it attacks", and because "they are very friendly, apart from at the airports"; a panther, because it is "clever and elegant, with finesse" and "has claws and strength but is a solitary animal"; a deer, because it is "majestic and audacious"; a fox, because it is cunning and "intelligent and in the right place at the right time. Also because they're ginger"; a unicorn, because it is "unique, it can't be compared to anyone or anything"; or a cat, because "they shit all over the place and do what they want".

An awkward neighbour

These characteristics, together with Britain's history and geography ("They are cut off from Europe. They are living there on that island"), helped account for the country's apparent attitude to its membership of the European Union. Essentially, "they don't like making agreements", "reject the idea of being part of a union" and have consequently "never been a proper part of the EU". Instead, having refused to sign up to Schengen and the single currency, the British have "one leg in and one leg out" or are "in Europe but not really part of the EU". Brits "just do their own thing. They're like Switzerland, but an island" or, as someone in Madrid put it, "they're the Catalans of the EU".

Several saw historical roots in the contrast between Britain's willingness to pursue its own interests openly and others' reluctance to seem too assertive. As one man in Dublin put it, "The difference is that the Germans are ashamed of what they've done and the British are proud, and they wave the flag." There was also a widespread view that Britain's true allegiances lay elsewhere: people in the UK still "drink juice from the colonies" and have closer ties to America (indeed, were "the Trojan Horse of the US in the EU", according to one of our Berlin participants).

Some took a dim view of Britain's approach. There was still "a bit too much Rule Britannia", and "they think they're a bit better. They're fine on their own so why do they have to follow the rules?" For these people, Britain was failing to live up to the European ideal: "When David Cameron is going into negotiations, his most common statement is 'What can we get out of Europe?' never 'What can we do for Europe?'"

Yet in every country we visited, people understood Britain's position as they saw it, and sympathised: "They make the calculation of what they pay and what they get, and they can see they are losing"; "They hold out, they bargain hard, they get the best. I've got no problem with it"; "For them it's more of a rational deal than an emotional one. I get it." Several suspected that Britain was losing patience with the high levels of migration that had resulted from the country's laudable openness to the world: "They are so open to different nationalities, they are too open and it has become too much for them. They have had immigration for so many years, maybe they have had enough."

> *"I wish we were more like the UK.*
> *We're just following the crowd."*

Not only that, many respected and even admired the way Britain conducted itself in Europe: "They see their opportunity and they fight. They hold onto their principles"; "They will bargain and bargain to the death but they will never make a decision unless they get 100 per cent of what they want"; "It shows power, strength, a personality." Moreover, Britain seemed to combine strength with a certain savvy, which had left it free of the constraints that other members had to tolerate: "They know things, they can sense things. They didn't want to join the Eurozone"; "It wasn't in their interests to join the currency union. They would have had 'sucker' painted on their foreheads in big letters if they'd joined the euro"; "They can alter their own interest rates!"

Indeed, our participants often said they wished their own

leaders would follow Britain's example, or that their country was in a position to do so: "It's impressive that they always seem to be in a strong position. We [in the Netherlands] could never leave the EU, but if the UK did they would have a chance of succeeding"; "Britain is independent, and that's good. They attend to their interests ... Maybe Poland should be more like that"; "I wish we were more like the UK. We're just following the crowd"; "Finally there is someone who stands up, gives the right example." As one man asked in Dublin, referring to the Taoiseach: "Can you imagine sending Enda in there? They believe they can do it. It's a big risk to take – if they don't, they could be out. There is a brashness – 'We're going to do it, and we'll still be in at the end of it.' But it could go either way. He's got a pair of balls going for a referendum, he really does."

In our poll, six in ten respondents in the other twenty-seven member states said they would rather see Britain remain in the EU; three in ten said it didn't matter either way, and just one in ten said they would prefer to see the UK leave. Lithuania, Malta, Portugal and Ireland were the keenest to keep Britain on board, while Austria, Cyprus, France and Luxembourg were happiest to show it the door. The youngest respondents, aged eighteen to twenty-four, were the most likely to want the UK to stay.

This balance was reflected in our focus groups. A few were content to see the troublesome British out of the way: "If it was France, we would be losing an ally, but England are cold. It is a neutral country that functions for its own sake"; "On the one hand, it would be a huge loss because they are a powerful country. On the other hand, if they don't want to be in it, then go"; "I'm indifferent. I don't like them anyway." But most wanted the UK to remain, for five broad reasons.

*"It's good to have them there to bring a bit more clarity
and less tomfoolery to what comes out of Brussels."*

First, as people in smaller, poorer countries readily admitted, "The UK is one of the countries that is giving the money"; "One rich country less in the EU would be bad for us." Second, "We may not be able to travel there. Maybe they will say, 'Let's throw out the seven hundred thousand Poles'"; "Would we [in Dublin] need a passport to go to Belfast?" Third, Brexit would leave the EU with less credibility and clout: "If a powerful player leaves the team, it will become weaker as a global player. We want the EU to be stronger in the world"; "The opinion of England matters internationally."

Fourth, Britain acted as a force for common sense and national sovereignty in Europe ("They limited the policymaking, so that's good"; "It's good to have them there to bring a bit more clarity and less tomfoolery to what comes out of Brussels"), and as a crucial counterweight to powers which would otherwise dominate: "It would upset the balance. We would be left with Germany doing whatever they want, without control. If England left, it would be a totally German union"; "I get restless when talking about the entry of the Turks and the exit of England."

*"It would upset the balance. We would be left with Germany
doing whatever they want, without control."*

Finally, without the UK there would simply be less point to the EU ("I feel like something would be missing … If Britain leaves, Europe won't mean anything any more"; "England has to be there, it has to be there. They're major league"). The EU would be a less desirable club to be a member of: "If Britain leaves, we'll be left behind with all these losers. Belgium!" Indeed,

Brexit would signal the failure of the European Union as an idea: it would be "the beginning of the end of the EU"; British departure would be "an inspiration for other countries", either (depending on your preference of leisure-based metaphor) causing a "domino effect" or leaving the union as "a house of cards". The EU needed the UK more than the reverse: "The Brits would be happy to be outside. But we don't want them to leave."

What's the bottom line?

Accordingly, most did not blame David Cameron for trying to negotiate a better deal for Britain ahead of the referendum. Some were grumpy about Britain further undermining the European ideal by demanding even better terms than it already enjoyed ("They have negotiated a lot of good things like their budget contributions. They are in a golden position"; "I don't agree we should say yes to all their whims. If they don't want to fit in they should leave") or suspected that they would end up paying one way or another: "I have the feeling that they are negotiating something at my expense." For a few, the British approach was just not cricket: "The UK is fighting for its citizens and its rights. If every country was doing that it wouldn't be possible to negotiate anything!"

> *"The UK is fighting for its citizens and its rights.*
> *If every country was doing that it wouldn't be*
> *possible to negotiate anything!"*

But, more often, the need to reach a compromise that would keep Britain in the union outweighed people's consternation. Indeed, some good might even come of it, especially if the negotiations produced reforms from which all would benefit. Not surprisingly, few people in the groups could name any of Britain's specific negotiating demands. When these were explained, most of them met little resistance and some were widely supported.

People in Eurozone countries were, perhaps understandably, nervous about guaranteeing that the UK would never contribute to euro bailouts (including some in France: "Who will help us when we're bankrupt?"), but cutting regulation, extending the single market, and more powers for national parliaments were largely uncontroversial ("Poland should submit something like this. See, the British are quite smart"). In our poll, no more than a quarter of EU respondents outside the UK thought any of these was unacceptable.

"How can you claim benefits for children who don't live there? Does that happen? Is it possible?"

The proposals which were expected to be most controversial in the negotiating room – insisting that EU migrants work and pay tax for four years before being eligible for certain benefits, and curbing their right to claim child benefit for children living abroad – were mostly seen by our focus groups as perfectly reasonable. People understood the pressure that welfare bills placed on the public finances ("They're trying to save their social budget. People go there just to get social security"), and many were surprised to hear the British system was so generous in comparison to their own: "How can you claim benefits for children who don't live there? Does that happen? Is it possible?"; "I think four years is too little. In Bulgaria it is five years." In any case, "Why should they get social welfare? They should go there and work."

Perhaps the most surprising finding was that, of all the items on Cameron's agenda, the one that met the most opposition was the most abstract: that idea that Britain should be exempt from the drive to create "ever closer union". Nearly four in ten of our EU-wide poll respondents rejected this demand, making it the only one for which the number disapproving equalled the number in favour. Respondents in Austria, Germany, Greece, Spain and Luxembourg were the most hostile. Participants in the groups also raised more objections to this proposal than to any of the more concrete items: "See, they don't want to be in"; "It's the original idea of the EU. It's counterproductive if one member state doesn't want to sign up to a basic principle. If they don't want to, they should leave"; "You can't want to be part of the union and not want it to be closer"; "What do they actually bring to Europe? When I hear their demands I wonder what Britain is doing there."

Two conclusions can be drawn from these findings. The first is that, had Cameron demanded more dramatic reforms, European politicians would, on the basis of this evidence, have encountered little domestic pressure to resist: the renegotiation might have secured bigger changes if Britain had asked for them.

> *"You can't want to be part of the union*
> *and not want it to be closer."*

The second is that, despite grumbles about the EU that would be familiar to British voters, many in Europe saw these things – daft rules and regulations, having to pay for other countries' economic problems, loss of national sovereignty – as part of the shared sacrifice necessary to a valuable common endeavour. Some regarded the project as an end in itself, or as the guarantee that Europe would not revert to the state of conflict that had been a perennial feature of continental affairs in their own lifetime or that of their parents. Those in the newer member states tended to see things more prosaically, in terms of the chance to work abroad, or access to financial support or new markets. But for them, the EU also signified their membership of the West and their arrival on the international stage. Even if the personal benefits had not lived up to what they felt had been promised, this gave rise to the basis of an emotional attachment to the EU itself that people in Britain tended not to share, even if they thought they were better off in than out.

That attachment was far from universal, as our survey showed. But it remained the case that most of Britain's fellow members had a different view of what they wanted the EU to be like – and there were twenty-seven of them, and only one UK.

APPENDIX TO CHAPTER II

The following findings are from You Should Hear What They Say About You, *our 28,000-sample EU-wide poll conducted in January and February 2016.*

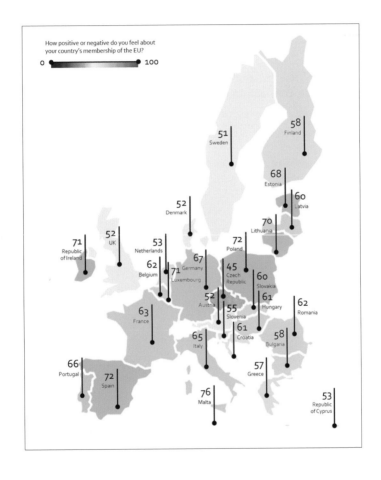

How positive or negative do you feel about your country's membership of the EU?

0 ▬▬▬▬▬▬▬▬ 100

51 Sweden
58 Finland
68 Estonia
60 Latvia
70 Lithuania
52 Denmark
52 UK
53 Netherlands
71 Republic of Ireland
72 Poland
67 Germany
62 Belgium
71 Luxembourg
45 Czech Republic
60 Slovakia
61 Hungary
62 Romania
52 Austria
63 France
55 Slovenia
61 Croatia
58 Bulgaria
65 Italy
57 Greece
66 Portugal
72 Spain
76 Malta
53 Republic of Cyprus

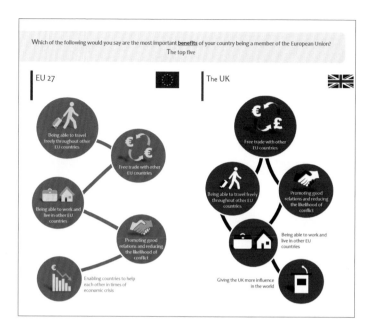

Which of the following would you say are the most important **benefits** of your country being a member of the European Union?
The top five

EU 27

- Being able to travel freely throughout other EU countries
- Free trade with other EU countries
- Being able to work and live in other EU countries
- Promoting good relations and reducing the likelihood of conflict
- Enabling countries to help each other in times of economic crisis

The UK

- Free trade with other EU countries
- Being able to travel freely throughout other EU countries
- Promoting good relations and reducing the likelihood of conflict
- Being able to work and live in other EU countries
- Giving the UK more influence in the world

Which of the following would you say are the most important **disadvantages** of your country being a member of the European Union?
The top five

EU 27

- The imposition of unnecessary rules and regulation
- Having to pay for other countries' economic problems
- Loss of national sovereignty
- Austerity imposed on us by the EU against our will
- The scale of immigration from other EU countries

The UK

- The scale of immigration from other EU countries
- Having to pay for other countries' economic problem
- The imposition of unnecessary rules and regulations
- Loss of national sovereignty
- The size of The UK's contribution to the EU budget

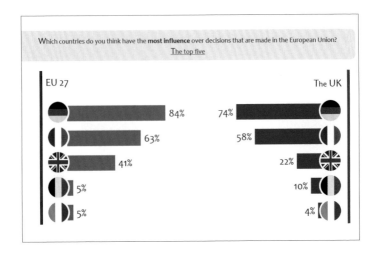

Which countries do you think have the **most influence** over decisions that are made in the European Union?

The top five

EU 27 / The UK

84% / 74%
63% / 58%
41% / 22%
5% / 10%
5% / 4%

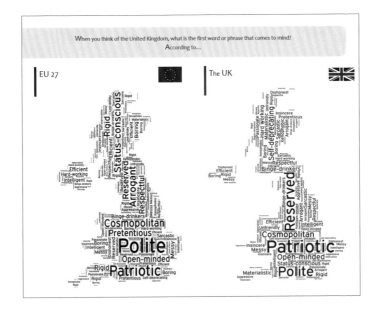

When you think of the United Kingdom, what is the first word or phrase that comes to mind?

According to...

EU 27 / The UK

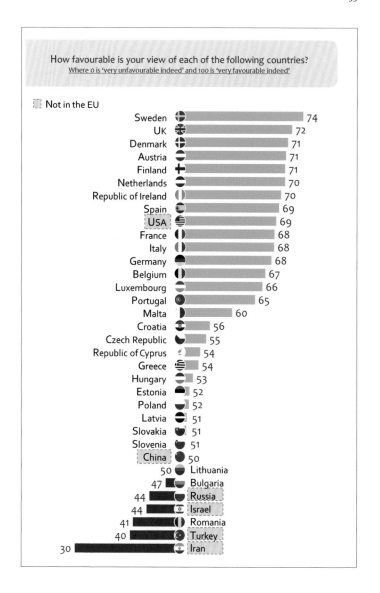

How favourable is your view of each of the following countries?
Where 0 is 'very unfavourable indeed' and 100 is 'very favourable indeed'

Not in the EU

Sweden	74
UK	72
Denmark	71
Austria	71
Finland	71
Netherlands	70
Republic of Ireland	70
Spain	69
USA	69
France	68
Italy	68
Germany	68
Belgium	67
Luxembourg	66
Portugal	65
Malta	60
Croatia	56
Czech Republic	55
Republic of Cyprus	54
Greece	54
Hungary	53
Estonia	52
Poland	52
Latvia	51
Slovakia	51
Slovenia	51
China	50
50	Lithuania
47	Bulgaria
44	Russia
44	Israel
41	Romania
40	Turkey
30	Iran

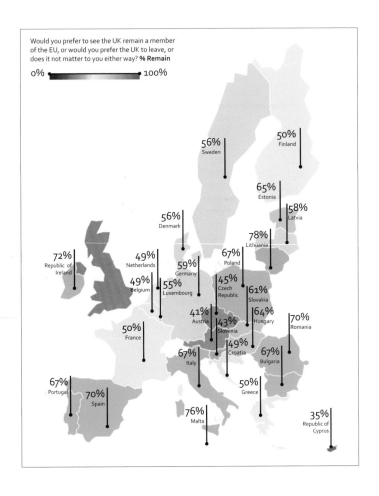

Would you prefer to see the UK remain a member of the EU, or would you prefer the UK to leave, or does it not matter to you either way? **% Remain**

0% ——————→ 100%

56% Sweden

50% Finland

65% Estonia

58% Latvia

56% Denmark

78% Lithuania

72% Republic of Ireland

49% Netherlands

59% Germany

67% Poland

49% Belgium

55% Luxembourg

45% Czech Republic

61% Slovakia

41% Austria

64% Hungary

70% Romania

50% France

43% Slovenia

49% Croatia

67% Bulgaria

67% Italy

50% Greece

67% Portugal

70% Spain

76% Malta

35% Republic of Cyprus

block unwanted legislation from Brussels. It would be recognised that the British government was solely responsible for the country's national security, meaning Britain would not join a European army. The changes would be legally binding in international law and would be deposited at the United Nations. In all, Cameron concluded, the deal was "enough for me to recommend that the United Kingdom remain in the European Union – having the best of both worlds". The country would be "stronger, safer and better off inside this reformed European Union". The following morning, after a rare weekend meeting of the cabinet, Cameron announced that the referendum would be held on Thursday 23 June. The vote would be "a once in a generation moment to shape the destiny of our country".

As well as launching the countdown to polling day, the conclusion of the renegotiation freed Conservative ministers to campaign on whichever side of the Brexit debate they wished. Six prominent ministers took this opportunity straight away: Michael Gove, the Justice Secretary; Chris Grayling, the Leader of the House of Commons; Theresa Villiers, the Northern Ireland Secretary; John Whittingdale, the Culture Secretary; and Priti Patel, who attended cabinet as an Employment Minister. Though they did not think the renegotiation had produced any significant change, they were careful not to blame Cameron: despite what Grayling described as his "herculean effort", the PM had discovered "the limitations of change that we can secure within the European Union", particularly when it came to giving Britain control of its own borders. The Fresh Start Group of Conservative MPs, which included several junior ministers, said that although the circumstances of the renegotiation had offered "the best chance for change in Europe we are likely to see for a generation", the reforms agreed fell far short of their hopes; most of the areas in which they had hoped to see changes – including social, regional, agricultural and criminal justice policy, and the Charter of Fundamental Rights – had not been addressed at all. Others pointed to a contrast between the outcome of the summit and what Cameron himself had said he wanted as far back as his Bloomberg speech in January 2013, including an end to child benefit payments for children of migrants who were not living in the UK, reforms to the Working Time Directive and better control of the EU budget.

As our research found at the end of 2015, when the government's putative negotiating demands were being feverishly debated by politicians and in the media, the details of what Cameron was seeking to achieve had barely registered with most people, though some had gathered that he wanted to change the rules on migrants' entitlement to welfare benefits. People generally supported this ambition, but most said they had little confidence that the PM would be able to win a better deal for Britain. Even so, more than one third of the population, including much higher numbers of Conservative-leaning undecideds, had said they would be more likely to vote to remain if he announced that he had secured better terms. The result, then, would turn less on the detail of the renegotiation Cameron had now secured than on his ability to sell the overall package.

A YouGov poll[4] conducted a few days after the summit's conclusion found just under half of the public claiming to have followed the story very or fairly closely (and this probably included a number giving themselves the benefit of the doubt). Only a quarter said that from what they had seen or heard, the result of the renegotiation was "a good deal for Britain",

4. YouGov poll, 21–23 February 2016, sample size 3,482.

while just over one third disagreed. Nearly four in ten said, or admitted, that they didn't know.

As the weeks passed and the debate moved on, so did the drama of the summit fade. In our research later in the campaign we asked undecided voters what they remembered of the renegotiation and its outcome. "Is that the one where he was up until eight a.m. and got an hour's kip and had to start again? I didn't hear anything about it after that," said one of our focus group participants at the end of April. Depending on people's view of Cameron, he had "gone in and batted for us, and did reasonably", or done it all as "window dressing ... He knew he wanted to stay in from the start, he had promised a referendum so he had to have one, so he had to come back and say he'd got a better deal."

> "He had promised a referendum so he had to have one,
> so he had to come back and say he'd got a better deal."

The prevailing view that was "he compromised, didn't he. He didn't get what he really wanted." In the great scheme of things, the changes that had resulted were "negligible". It had not been a turning point in the campaign, at least not of the kind that the remain side might have hoped. As much as it showed a Prime Minister battling for Britain, the episode had reminded people that defending the country's interests in Europe often meant having a scrap, which we didn't always win: "They walked all over us. They got their way again."

Still, the remain campaign might have exploited the renegotiation more successfully than they managed to do. Discussing the remain "pledge card" two weeks before polling day, one of our participants alighted on the promise of "a special status in Europe". "I'm not sure what that one means," he said. "But if that counteracts some of the arguments for leave, let's hear it." Well, what if we could be part of the single market, have free movement of people albeit with migration to the UK, stay out of the euro, not be part of the Schengen no-borders area, and not have to contribute to Eurozone bailouts or accept migrant quotas? "Better," came the response. "Brexit-lite." "But what's the likelihood of having something like that?"

Follow the money

However pleased Number Ten really were with the Brussels deal, they knew a campaign based on Britain's bright new future in Europe would be a tough sell. Rather than try to extol the benefits of staying, the remain side decided to focus on the risks of leaving – above all, the risks to the economy. In April, the Treasury published what the Chancellor, George Osborne, described as a "serious and sober assessment of the economic facts". This concluded that if the UK left the EU and instead had a negotiated bilateral relationship like Canada's, the country's GDP would be 6.2 per cent lower by 2030. The average family would be £4,300 worse off than under continued membership, and tax receipts would be £36 billion lower – the equivalent of more than a third of the NHS budget, or eight pence on the basic rate of income tax.

As our focus groups found, this claim found its way through to the voters, some of whom found it worrying ("Well, it's a lot of money for any household, isn't it?"). At the same time, people were not sure whether to believe it: "Where have they got that random figure?" The Treasury dossier might be full of scholarly equations, but "you can make statistics tell you anything". Some were wary of any government prediction: "He can't

even forecast for two years correctly, never mind fifteen years."
A poll[5] by Ipsos MORI the week before referendum day found
seven in ten thinking the claim that households would lose
£4,300 per year and be permanently poorer if Britain voted to
leave was false; only 17 per cent said they believed it.

"The Chancellor was on the news this morning throwing his toys
out of the pram and saying he was going to make us suffer."

Later in the campaign, Osborne warned that Brexit would
cause an instant "DIY recession" which could last a year and
cost over eight hundred thousand jobs; Cameron said leaving
the EU would be like "putting a bomb under the economy",
triggering "a decade of uncertainty". The remain side warned
of higher prices, lower incomes, more expensive holidays,
smaller pensions, less money for public services and falling
house prices (the last of which sounded to aspiring first-time
buyers like rather good news). A week before polling day,
Osborne threatened an emergency budget to raise taxes and
cut spending in order to fill the black hole in the public finances that he said would result from a decision to leave ("The
Chancellor was on the news this morning throwing his toys
out of the pram and saying he was going to make us suffer," as
one of our participants put it).

If such claims could be dismissed or at least discounted
as campaign rhetoric, they were echoed by bodies like the
International Monetary Fund, which in April forecast "severe
regional and global damage" in the event of the UK's exit. Two
weeks later, the OECD declared that Brexit would cost British
people the equivalent of a month's salary by 2020, and in May,

5. Ipsos MORI June 2016 Political Monitor, 11–14 June 2016, sample 1,257.

Christine Lagarde, the IMF's managing director, described the outlook for Britain outside the EU as "pretty bad to very, very bad".

Yet many voters refused to take even these interventions at face value. Being a European herself, and a member of the global elite, Madame Lagarde would be "more concerned about what's going to happen to the rest of them" than what was best for Britain. The priority for an international body like the IMF would be to keep existing structures in place: "A lot of them have vested interests, especially the rest of Europe. They are having trouble with Greece, Cyprus, Portugal – if Britain leaves they'll turn around and say, 'Well, we'll leave too.'" In any case, like the Treasury, "historically the IMF have got a lot of things wrong, so I'm not convinced. The idea that we're going to end up on our own doing nothing is nonsense." A warning from Roberto Azevêdo, head of the World Trade Organization, that British consumers would pay billions in trade tariffs outside the EU met a similar reception: "He's not going to be short of a penny or two. He's probably looking at big business, but if you look at small ones, they say the EU costs them more and causes them problems." Nor were our groups impressed when Emmanuel Macron, the French Economy Minister, pronounced that, outside the EU, Britain would be "completely killed" in trade talks with China: "He wants us to stay in because it benefits his country." If the UK leaves, "the ninety-litre booze cruise comes to an end". Indeed, this was the response to any intervention from a European politician: they would "lose all that money" if Britain left, and other countries might follow suit. Many thought "they need us more than we need them".

"Obama is not looking after our interests but US interests."

When it came to advice from visiting dignitaries, the biggest raspberry of all was reserved for Barack Obama. At a joint press conference with Cameron during his visit to Britain at the end of April, the President said a trade deal between the UK and the United States was "not going to happen any time soon because our focus is in negotiating with a big bloc, the European Union, to get a trade agreement done". He added that "the UK is going to be in the back of the queue".

If the remain camp had hoped this would prove a decisive intervention, they were to be disappointed. Though some in our groups were worried, rather more were indignant at Obama "sticking his oar in". Obama was trying to "bully" Britain into continuing to share sovereignty in a way the United States itself would never do, and not because he had Britain's welfare at heart: "America prefers to do deals with big regional blocs. So he's not looking after our interests but US interests"; "It came across as almost childish. 'If you don't do what we want, we're not going to play with you.'" In any case, "He's not in office for long, is he?"

Business leaders were not a great deal more help, for two reasons. First, they undeniably had a vested interest: "It might be good for you to stay, but that doesn't mean it's good for us." And, second, it seemed that for each one who thought we were better off in (Sir Richard Branson, Sir Martin Sorrell, Lord Sugar), another thought we were better off out (Sir James Dyson, Lord Bamford, "the guy who owns the chain of pubs"). "There are a lot of business surveys but you can prove anything with statistics. It's X per cent of top companies think this, then the next week it's X per cent say there are more opportunities from leaving"; "You get one great businessman on one side, and another on the other, so who the hell do you go with?"

The same applied for those whose own employers had

written to them about the referendum. One said their boss had urged them to vote to remain "but I don't really trust him. And so did the union. But I don't really feel it was for them to push their opinion on me." Not everyone objected in principle to employers having a view, but ultimately "it's my opinion that matters. It's about what I want."

> *"You get one great businessman on one side,*
> *and another on the other,*
> *so who the hell do you go with?"*

The leave campaign was not immune to questions about its own figures. People felt that small businesses were less enthused by EU membership than large ones, but our participants questioned the claim that Brussels regulations cost them £600 million every week: "I don't know where they get those figures. How many billion billions would that be over ten years?"

The Neutrality Paradox

Part of the problem was that the economic arguments felt complicated, and the two sides seemed directly to contradict each other. To pick one issue and one day, on 24 March, Energy Secretary Amber Rudd claimed that leaving the EU could add millions of pounds to household energy costs; Andrea Leadsom, a fellow Energy Minister, countered that Brexit would free the UK from expensive European legislation and lead to cheaper bills. Since people felt they had no means of judging between what sounded like complicated technical arguments, many were left feeling bewildered: "It's like watching *Match of the Day*. A player has gone down in the box, and two ex-professionals can't agree if he's dived or not, and if they can't decide, how's the referee supposed to decide? And the referee is us."

> *"It's like watching* Match of the Day. *A player has gone down in the box, and two ex-professionals can't agree if he's dived or not, and if they can't decide, how's the referee supposed to decide? And the referee is us."*

Confusion was particularly acute when it came to the single market – indeed, we found that by no means everyone was sure what this term even meant. In our Europe-wide poll, UK respondents named "free trade with other EU countries" as the main benefit of membership, and the fact that 44 per cent of UK exports went to Europe was one of the remain campaign's consistent themes. But many voters struggled to understand why this could not still be the case after Brexit. If trade was to the benefit of both parties, surely it was as much in our partners' interests for it to continue as our own. "They're saying if we opt out, we're not going to be able to trade. That's a big lie"; "They say there'll be tariffs when we buy champagne from France, and on whatever we get from Italy. Pasta, I suppose. But I don't think there will"; "Why would they stop trading with us? The links are still there." Some feared the EU would make life difficult for Britain as a punishment for leaving and to encourage other countries to stay, but others thought pragmatism would prevail: "No one bloody likes America and they manage to trade. I don't see why we would have so many problems."

> *"No one bloody likes America and they manage to trade. I don't see why we would have so many problems."*

What people needed, they said, was guidance from impartial experts who would cut through the claims and counterclaims and identify "the facts" (or "a wee list of the pros and cons", as one of our Belfast participants put it). This was a forlorn hope, and not just because no facts were available about the future. The other difficulty was what we named the Neutrality Paradox, a concept neatly illustrated by the Institute for Fiscal Studies, which produced a report in May suggesting that Brexit would damage the public finances, prolonging austerity by two years. Here was an organisation respected for its rigorous independent analysis of economic issues, giving its considered view. The reaction? "There's the report from these experts, someone all the parties regard as experts, who say we need to stay in. So even there, they're chucking in what side they want you to go for." A neutral body has given its analysis, the analysis points to one outcome being more favourable than the other, ergo it is not neutral.

> *"I don't think anyone is completely independent,*
> *but somehow Mark Carney's view is less biased.*
> *Maybe it's because he's Canadian."*

Our research identified two individuals who came close to the status of trusted expert witness. The first was Mark Carney, the Governor of the Bank of England. Carney did not sound impartial, exactly: he identified Brexit as the biggest domestic risk to the UK economy and warned of instability, interest rate rises and even recession (for which he was criticised by MPs campaigning for a leave vote). Yet his warnings somehow seemed to carry more weight than those of the campaigners: "MPs take their advice from the Governor of the Bank of England so his advice is worth taking on something like this";

"I don't think anyone is completely independent, but somehow his view is less biased. Maybe it's because he's Canadian." His nationality meant he was unlikely to have been a member of the Bullingdon Club or to be bound by the obligations of the old school tie. Also he "seems like a nice man" and had the important virtue of being "not a politician". But then again, "Would the government let him say anything they didn't like?"

> *"I really hate my job. I would love to go in tomorrow and say*
> *I'm going to leave and become an actor. I could become*
> *the next Doctor Who. Or I could fall flat on my face and*
> *lose my pension. It's the same with the referendum.*
> *Do I want to take the risk of it all going tits up?"*

The other person whose credentials compelled people's attention was Martin Lewis, famous to millions as the Money Saving Expert: "He's good. He tells you as it is"; "He gives you the facts"; "I trust what he says more than anyone else." In early June, he released a video in which he explained that "there are no facts" – which, as well as reassuring viewers that they had not missed something important, helped expose the shrill assertions from the rival campaigns: "So how does Cameron know 100 per cent, or Farage?" Lewis's conclusion, that he felt leaving the EU carried the greater risk and uncertainty, clearly chimed with several in the groups: "If I had to vote now, after watching that, I think I'd stay in." This was perhaps all the more the case because of his insistence that he was not campaigning (which also helped him avoid the Neutrality Paradox). His balance-of-risk approach also hit home: "I really hate my job. I would love to go in tomorrow and say I'm going to leave and become an actor. I could become the next Doctor Who. Or I could fall flat on my face and lose my pension.

It's the same with the referendum. Do I want to take the risk of it all going tits up?"

Throughout 2016, YouGov's regular tracking survey[6] found more people thinking leaving the EU would make Britain worse off economically than that it would make the country better off (indeed, not since 2013 had people given the opposite answer, and by only a tiny margin). In the five months before referendum day, the gap widened from five points to fifteen, but the pessimists were outweighed by the consistent quarter of voters who thought Brexit would make no difference, and the further one in five or so who said they didn't know. Towards the end of the campaign, the company found[7] just over one third of respondents saying they thought the remain campaign's claims about the effect of Brexit on the economy were *wildly exaggerated and have little or no truth behind them*. But two fifths thought either that the claims were exaggerated *but the points they make are basically true*, or that the claims *are realistic and true, and they are not exaggerating*. A further one in five didn't know what to think.

"What happens if you can't struggle for two years? ... People have this mentality about 'we are Britain', but it's a load of rubbish. When they say 'take our country back', what do they **mean?**"

This reflected the balance of opinion in our focus groups of undecided voters. Even most of those inclined to vote to leave expected that the economy would take a hit in the short term, or perhaps for a number of years, if only because of the prolonged uncertainty that Brexit would entail: "There will be a slump at first. The pound won't be as strong. That's a given";

6. YouGov EU Referendum Trackers – see YouGov.com.
7. YouGov poll, 9–10 June 2016, sample 1,671.

"Both sides say it will be grim for two years. That's the only thing they can agree on." The question, then, was whether this would be a price worth paying to be, as they saw it, liberated from the European Union. For some, the answer was an emphatic no: they were not prepared to endure real hardship for what they regarded as abstract ideas about sovereignty and control: "What happens if you can't struggle for two years? Last time we had a recession, the construction industry was hit, salaries were affected"; "People have this mentality about 'we are Britain', but it's a load of rubbish. When they say 'take our country back', what do they *mean*?"

But for a determined section of voters, warnings about a few pounds a week in take-home pay, or a few extra months of austerity, were as nothing compared to the bigger issues at stake. The economy would have its ups and downs inside or outside the EU ("In my lifetime we've had two recessions and I didn't lose any weight in either of them"), and what was a bit more spending restraint in the great scheme of things? "It would be acceptable to me, that. Two years, and then we'd be back where we are now, basically. Two years' austerity, and then you get your freedom."

Who's in charge here?

This freedom for Britain to run its own affairs was at the heart of the leave campaign, summed up in its slogan, "Vote Leave, Take Control". In February, YouGov found[8] nearly two fifths saying one of the three worst things about EU membership was that the union had *interfered too much in how member*

8. YouGov poll, 21–23 February 2015, sample 3,482.

countries run their affairs. Conservative supporters and undecided referendum voters were more likely to think of this as
a downside of EU membership than high levels of migration
from Eastern Europe. With some success, the leave camp
consistently underlined this message with examples of how
Britain had lost control of its own affairs. A dossier on Europe's
powers to prevent the UK deporting foreign criminals, for
example, drew the reaction the campaign would have hoped
for from our focus groups: "The EU has got so many ridiculous
laws and regulations. The out party is saying we can dispense
with the nonsense that comes out of Brussels and get back to
common sense."

"What does this 'Brex' word mean?"

One reason the theme was so effective was that it was hard to
counter on its own terms. Sir John Major made a valiant attempt
to do so, arguing that in today's world, complete control was
an illusion, concluding, "If you want undiluted sovereignty in
the modern age when everybody is interconnected, then go to
North Korea." But this argument proved too abstract for many
of our undecided voters: if it was easy to grasp the concept of
taking control, reflections on the nature of sovereignty in the
modern age were a step too far: "I don't get any of that," said
someone in our focus groups. "Nigel Farage was at least at
my level of understanding. It's well over my head, the kind of
words they're using"; "You need to talk on my terms. I don't
like politics, I don't know about it. All of that, I thought,
I don't actually know what he's going on about."

(This was by no means the only complaint of this kind.
People in our groups often said they felt defeated by the elev-
ated arguments and the jargon: "There are not personal enough

questions about how it will affect you as an individual … The crux is that I don't know if it really matters to me. I can't see it. In local elections I have strong views about how it will affect me but I can't relate to this." Someone would regularly ask, "What does this 'Brex' word mean?")

> *"The crux is that I don't know if it really matters to me.*
> *I can't see it. In local elections I have strong views about*
> *how it will affect me but I can't relate to this."*

Our own poll[9] in May tried to clarify the sovereignty question. Just over six in ten, including seven out of ten Conservative voters, thought *we must have more control over our own affairs even if that means missing out on some of the benefits of co-operating with other countries.* Most Liberal Democrat voters and 18–24-year-olds, by contrast, thought *we must be prepared to give away some control over our own affairs in return for getting the benefits of co-operating with other countries.* SNP voters (perhaps conscious of a potential contradiction with other parts of their political outlook) were evenly divided, as were Labour voters.

> *"If we got out, we would be stuck with a Tory government. At*
> *least if we're in the EU, it's not solely them making the decisions."*

For our focus group participants, the most powerful argument against "taking control" was not that it was impossible but that it would be a bad thing to do. However exasperating some European rules might be, they included some good ones – particularly on workers' rights, about which David Cameron published a rare joint piece with Brendan Barber,

9. Lord Ashcroft Polls, EU referendum survey, 13–18 May 2016, sample 5,009.

former General Secretary of the Trades Union Congress, in the *Guardian* two months before the referendum. Such rights, some reflected, might never have been instituted by a British government, or at least not a Conservative one: "One thing I really like about Europe is the protection of the worker. I'm just worried that they'll squeeze the workers if we fall into a recession. Workers do need protection." Without the EU to enforce these rights, they might start to disappear, "slowly but surely, maybe one at a time, so to speak ... We could be following in American footsteps."

"If we're going to balls the country up let's do it ourselves, not let somebody else do it."

For some, the fear of Westminster having more power went beyond the question of employment legislation: "If we got out, we would be stuck with a Tory government. At least if we're in the EU, it's not solely them making the decisions"; "The ability to make our own decisions, I don't see that as a positive. If you look at what goes on in the House of Commons, it's disgusting. They just try to get one over on each other. We would have no appeal to the Court of Human Rights. It would mean what David Cameron says goes, and if you want to change that, tough shit."

Migration matters

For those who felt strongly that the UK should have the right to make more of its own decisions (or at least that "if we're going to balls the country up let's do it ourselves, not let somebody else do it"), the principle would need to be exercised first and foremost on the question of immigration. As noted in the previous chapter, British voters considered the scale of migration from EU countries the biggest single downside of membership, and polls throughout the campaign found immigration competing with economic issues as the most important practical questions at stake in the referendum. This point was neatly illustrated by a YouGov survey[10] in February, which found that people divided almost precisely between those who would rather Britain had *full control over immigration from Europe, but British businesses no longer having free access to trade with the EU,* and those who would prefer the reverse.

Sovereignty and immigration amounted to the twin themes of the leave campaign, at least when measured by what the voters heard. As we saw in our survey in May, in which we asked people to say without being prompted what messages they had picked up from the leave camp, "border control" and "control over laws" dominated the responses.

The leave side kept the question of immigration close to the top of the agenda throughout the campaign. In April, Michael Gove warned of an "immigration free-for-all" if Britain remained in the EU, with migrants from new member states posing a "direct and serious threat" to public services. In May, Boris Johnson argued that the government's target of cutting net migration to below one hundred thousand would be impossible to achieve inside the EU (something which Steve Hilton, Cameron's former adviser, later claimed the Prime Minister had been told by civil servants; Downing Street denied this), and Gove claimed that the population would grow by an extra five million if the UK remained a member. In June, the leave campaign proposed an Australian-style points system, and Priti Patel, the Employment Minister, wrote

10. YouGov poll, 21–23 February 2016, sample 3,482.

an article claiming that "those leading the pro-EU campaign" – implying, but not naming, Cameron and Osborne – were not concerned about the consequences of migration for working people because, for them, it was "pretty much all gain and no pain: inexpensive domestic help, willing tradesmen and convenient, cheap travel".

"Yesterday, my boss, when her child didn't get into the school she wanted, she said, 'That's it, I'm out.'"

Events helped the leave campaign in their efforts. During the campaign, Oxford University's Migration Observatory reported that the Eurozone crisis was encouraging more southern European migrants to head to the UK to join those from the East. The Office for National Statistics published figures showing that 1.2 million more EU migrants had been given National Insurance numbers in the last five years than had shown up in the immigration figures, that net migration had risen to 333,000, including 184,000 from elsewhere in the EU, and that around three million people in the UK were citizens of another EU country, with European migrants making up 6.8 per cent of the British workforce. Reports from southern Europe, where people continued to arrive by boat from Africa and the Middle East, were a continuous theme in the daily news.

Immigration was a constant concern among people in our focus groups. Very often, this was related to competition for school places and other public services: "In the school where I teach, about 88 per cent have English as a second language. As a mum, I think of all those children fighting for a place. Although I'm still more 'in' than 'out', that might tip the balance for me"; "Yesterday, my boss, when her child didn't get into the school she wanted, she said, 'That's it, I'm out.'"

Hearing Boris Johnson warn that Britain's population could rise to eighty million, people thought, "He's got a point. We're an island. We can't take all these people."

For all the drama of the new migration figures, their effect was more to keep the story going than to add a dramatic new twist – though they did highlight the government's failure to cut net migration to the tens of thousands. Some even thought that the numbers put things in perspective: "It's not as high as you imagine. The way the media portrays it you'd think it was millions coming in every year."

> "I think it's a lot higher than three million, a lot higher. There are probably three million in Yorkshire alone."

Still, many assumed that Britain's "open-door policy" for EU citizens must mean that the "vast majority" of total immigration into the UK came from fellow member states. And "it's constantly on the news about how many are coming in from Europe so I'd have thought it was more from Europe than from outside".

As is often the case with political statistics, people were not always prepared to take the data at face value, either for annual arrivals or for the total: "If that's the registered number, what's the real number?"; "I think it's a lot higher than three million, a lot higher. There are probably three million in Yorkshire alone." And whatever the true figure, "the scariest thing is the trend. If you add ten years, that could add twenty million to the UK. They don't have two or three kids, they have five or six. And so will their kids." The principle of having full control over Britain's immigration policy seemed unarguable to many: "It would be our choice. We could calibrate it according to the country's needs."

Few who were worried about immigration were reassured by Theresa May's insistence that Britain already controlled its borders. We were not able to decide who could and could not come to live in the UK, they argued, and there were plenty of examples of Europeans entering the country with criminal records and going on to commit crimes. Indeed, some thought they detected that the Home Secretary was supporting the remain campaign only "through gritted teeth ... I suspect there are politicians that aren't too certain. Theresa May is one of them, definitely."

Perhaps the most controversial element in the immigration debate was the strong suggestion from the leave campaign that Turkey was on the verge of joining, increasing the EU's population (and therefore the numbers eligible to come to Britain) by some eighty million. Defence Minister and leave campaigner Penny Mordaunt said Turkey was due to accede within eight years and that the UK would have no say on the question. David Cameron fiercely rebutted both claims, pointing out that all member states have a veto over new members and saying that Turkey was currently on course to join "in about the year 3,000". Still, the waters were muddied. A poll[11] by Ipsos MORI the week before the referendum found the public divided over the truth of the claim that *Turkey will be fast-tracked into the European Union and their population of 75 million people will have the right to free movement to the UK* (45 per cent thought it was true, 45 per cent thought it false).

> "If we stay in and Turkey joins the EU, there are millions of
> Turks who want to come to the UK. It really worries me.
> Will they have jobs? Will they have their own money?
> Will they have private health care? I don't think so."

11. Ipsos MORI June 2016 Political Monitor, 11–14 June 2016, sample 1,257.

In our groups, some had the impression that Turkish membership was imminent, and were concerned: "The immigration thing will explode. If we stay in and Turkey joins the EU, there are millions of Turks who want to come to the UK. It really worries me. Will they have jobs? Will they have their own money? Will they have private health care? I don't think so." Moreover, Europe's need for Turkish co-operation over the migrant crisis seemed to have given Ankara more bargaining chips: "Hasn't it speeded up because of the deal they've done with the migrants? They're saying if they don't let them into the EU, they'll let the border down." And as for a British veto, "I find it hard to believe one country would go against twenty-seven others. It would be a very brave country."

Apart from the potential migrant numbers, the question of Turkish accession troubled our undecided voters for two more reasons. One was security: "It's a dual-continent country, it has a border with Syria. We would be more susceptible to terrorist attacks"; "They've got a lot of migrants from Syria who are supposed to claim asylum in the first country, which is Turkey, and then they take on Turkish nationality and they can go where they like." The other was that it underlined another of the leave campaign's arguments – that by voting to remain in the EU we would not be choosing the status quo: "When we joined, it was six countries, a completely different animal." This prompted some in our groups to see the balance of risk between staying and leaving in a different way.

> *"Would there be a border back up at Newry?*
> *Will we need a passport to go down south?"*

The question of free movement had an extra dimension in Northern Ireland. Indeed, this was the first potential consequence of leaving the EU that our Belfast groups thought of: "Would there be a border back up at Newry? Will we need a passport to go down south?" As things stood, they only noticed they had crossed the border "because the signs change from miles to kilometres", but some feared that Brexit would bring the prospect of passport control, customs, security checks and everything else associated with an international frontier. Trade with the south might also suffer if the UK found itself outside the single market: "We would be exporting to another country."

> *"There's an ugly group who want to come out for ugly reasons, who say 'they' are responsible for all the problems in the country and 'they' should stop coming in. It's rearing its head at every opportunity."*

Three things held immigration back from being an even more important factor than it was. One was that many of our undecided voters thought the issue had so dominated the leave campaign that they wondered if it was the only argument they had. Many did not want to vote on immigration alone, even if they thought it was important. Another was that people did not always like the tone in which they heard the subject discussed. This view was not confined to social media, but was aired in our groups: "Nigel Farage and his lot don't separate migration, immigration, asylum seekers, illegal immigrants – they lump them all together." There was "an ugly group who want to come out for ugly reasons, who say 'they' are responsible for all the problems in the country and 'they' should stop coming in. It's rearing its head at every opportunity."

A speech by Nigel Farage in which he mentioned the events in Cologne on New Year's Eve and warned of the consequences

of introducing to Britain large numbers of males "from countries where women are, at best, second class citizens" was, for
some, a case in point: "That was horrific. The stupidity of the
man, saying if we stay in the EU we're all going to be raped in
the street." This reaction was by no means universal, however;
others in our groups, both men and women, thought he had
raised an uncomfortable truth, as he often did ("I like a bit
of Nige").

③ The third reason why immigration did not always sway the
votes of those who thought it an important issue was that they
often doubted that leaving the EU would make any difference.
A YouGov poll[12] in June found that while nearly seven in ten
voters thought immigration from EU countries was too high,
fewer than half thought it would fall if Britain were to leave,
and only one in five believed it would "go down a lot".

Our groups helped explain why people did not automat-
ically equate Brexit with less migration. For one thing, "half
comes from the EU and half from the rest of the world. If we've
got control over that half, why aren't we controlling it more?
If we can't do it now, why would we do it after?" Leaving the
EU could also mean "we won't have that relationship with
France, so the camp at Calais might come to England because
we couldn't have our border control there". If we wanted a
free-trade deal with Europe after our departure, free movement would probably have to continue too: "That's one of the
conditions they'll make us do."

> *"Latvians and Poles are doing jobs that people
> here don't want to do ... Who wants to go
> picking lettuces and things like that?"*

12. YouGov poll, 9–10 June 2016, sample 1,671.

A lso

Since nobody in the leave campaign seemed to be suggesting that migrants already in Britain should be asked to leave (and nobody in our groups thought this should happen), the pressures would continue: "Even if we were out, the housing is already gone. A Tory won't do anything about that." And whether we were in or out, migrants would continue to arrive because we needed them: "Latvians and Poles are doing jobs that people here don't want to do … Who wants to go picking lettuces and things like that?"

How to spend it

Alongside sovereignty and border control, the third pillar of the leave campaign was the financial cost of Britain's EU membership. The claim that the UK sent £350 million a week to Brussels, which featured on the side of the Vote Leave battle bus, was at least as contentious as the assertion that Turkey was on the verge of joining the union. The figure was gross, not net, meaning that it included money that came back to the UK in various forms, and took no account of Britain's rebate, which, the remain camp protested, was deducted from the fee and never sent to Europe in the first place. Sir Andrew Dilnot, chair of the UK Statistics Authority, described the figure as "potentially misleading", and the Institute for Fiscal Studies concluded that the cost of membership amounted to £8 billion a year, rather than the £20 billion that the leave camp claimed.

"It's the amount it costs that worries me.
It is something like ten billion a day? Or is it ten million?
Or seven million. Anyway, I was shocked when I heard."

Despite the controversy – or more likely, because of it – the £350 million number was one of the few figures to stick in voters' minds throughout the campaign. Our focus group participants nearly always mentioned it spontaneously. Even if they could not remember the number, they knew it was something enormous: "It's the amount it costs that worries me. It is something like ten billion a day? Or is it ten million? Or seven million. Anyway, I was shocked when I heard."

Though people knew by referendum day that the figure was heavily disputed, the cost of membership had become an issue for many voters and was one of the three clearest messages they remembered from the leave side. Ipsos MORI found[13] in June that nearly eight in ten voters had heard that Britain sent £350 million a week to the EU, and just under half believed it was true. The same survey found that the leave campaign's claim that this cost would rise in the future as Britain was forced to contribute to Eurozone bailouts was more likely to be believed than disbelieved.

The implication of the leave message was that if we no longer had to send all this money to Brussels, we could spend it on our own priorities instead. Indeed, they defended their use of the gross rather than the net figure for Britain's contribution on the grounds that European officials were deciding how much came back to the UK, where it was spent, and on what. But although people were ready to be outraged by the amount of money their government sent to Europe, they were far from certain that they would see any benefit if the funds stayed at home.

*"If anyone thinks they would really spend it
on the NHS, they need their head examined."*

13. Ipsos MORI June 2016 Political Monitor, 11–14 June 2016, sample 1,257.

Voters were especially doubtful of the suggestion – also emblazoned on the Brexit battle bus – that if Britain were to leave the EU, much of the £350 million would be used to "fund the NHS instead". To our undecided voters, this seemed much too good to be true: "If anyone thinks they would really spend it on the NHS, they need their head examined. It would go on tax cuts for businesses and getting rid of the deficit, not schools and hospitals." In fact, as YouGov found in their tracking surveys[14] throughout 2016, people were consistently more likely to think leaving the EU would be good for the NHS than to think it would be bad – but our groups suggested this owed more to the perceived burden of EU migration on the health service than to the expectation of a post-Brexit financial windfall.

In parts of the country that had benefited from EU funding, some thought they might lose out if spending decisions were all made at home. Nor were they much comforted by assurances from the leave campaign that, as Priti Patel put it, there would be "more than enough money" to go around after Brexit. Europe had often stepped in where Westminster had not, they felt, and they doubted that any losses would be made up: "When I think of European money, I think of the Metro extension to the airport, and the quayside," a man in Newcastle reflected. "London has a very poor record of investing in the North East, but Europe has invested."

Our groups in Cardiff believed Wales had done well out of European funds for infrastructure and agriculture ("You never see a poor farmer, do you?") and, if the money were being handed out from London, "I think less money would find itself in Wales than in parts of England." The same view

14. YouGov EU Referendum Trackers – see YouGov.com.

emerged in Cornwall, where people in our groups had seen European funding for social projects, new roads and fibre-optic broadband, and feared that when it came to national priorities, "We're a bit of a forgotten county. We're just seen as a holiday place."

In Northern Ireland, the EU had spent over £1 billion since 1995 on its Peace Programme, but people in our Belfast focus groups could only guess what this entailed ("What does that mean? New flags?") They were more aware of agricultural subsidies and transport projects, and were pleased to hear about a £5 million investment in new buses ("We do get through them quite a bit here. Buses are not what you'd call a fixed asset in Belfast"). Would this continue if the UK were outside the EU? "You'd like to think so, but it depends what type of government we have at Westminster." Northern Ireland was sometimes "a bit of a poor relation. Most of the money would go back to England. I'm not sure we wouldn't get any. But we certainly wouldn't get as much."

World War Three?

In a competitive field, perhaps the most notorious claim from either side came in David Cameron's speech on 9 May, in which he said that Britain's departure from the EU could risk undermining "peace and stability on our continent" – or, as the *Daily Mail* had it, that "Brexit would lead to war and genocide". The warning was heard by our undecided voters, who roundly mocked it. Though there might well be a case to be made for co-operating with our neighbours on security matters, this sounded rather desperate: "Apparently if we leave, the sky is going to fall in and World War Three is going to break out"; "Is that trying to frighten us, saying we're in danger of being attacked by the Russians? He's just throwing everything into the pot"; "Next they'll say we're going to be attacked by extra-terrestrials."

Having watched extracts from the PM's speech, some in our groups felt he had been more measured than the headlines, though this may have been calculated: "Cameron isn't exactly saying World War Three, it has been blown up a bit. But he's happy for it to be blown up. He can say, 'I didn't say that, but...'" And a few admitted it had worried them, despite the obvious hyperbole: "Part of me thinks it's rubbish but I'm a mum of three, one of my family wants to join the army, and looking at history and things that have happened before – you think, oh my goodness, if there's a war, and it all starts going round in your head"; "Are you sure you want to gamble with the Russians?"

> *"Apparently if we leave, the sky is going to fall in and World War Three is going to break out."*

But for most people, including many who were otherwise leaning towards voting to remain, the security argument did not hold water. For one thing, the EU seemed irrelevant in this field: "It's NATO and our own defence that's the main thing in security. This isn't the main reason I would stay in or vote out." For another thing, when the EU had faced challenges to peace and security in the past, it had failed abysmally: "When there have been things on the border with Europe, like the former Yugoslavia, Europe failed to act even though there was genocide"; "Russia annexed Crimea and Europe did bugger all"; "The EU is like a pitbull with no teeth." It also seemed odd to cite the EU as a source of protection when it came to the migrant crisis, when "Angela Merkel said they could all come in, so she partly caused it". Worse still, free movement for European citizens surely made it harder to counter the terror threat.

Above all, it seemed to the groups that the dangers Britain faced would be identical whether we were part of the EU or not ("someone like Russia or ISIS are not going to say, 'OK, we'll leave you alone if you stay in'"). Membership had not prevented terrorist attacks in European cities, and seemed irr-elevant to the global security situation: "Iraq and Afghanistan had nothing to do with Europe ... the threats we face are from around the African continent, from dissident Irish terrorists, our intelligence partners are Saudi Arabia, Turkey, the US..." As for the need to share intelligence with other EU countries, "The idea that we're not going to tell each other things because we're not part of the club is nonsense." Published polls sup-ported this: while similar numbers thought we would be safer inside and outside the EU, voters were most likely to think it made no difference to Britain's national security either way.

At the end of May, it emerged that a policy paper setting out steps towards the creation of a European army were being held back until after the referendum, apparently to avoid alarming British voters. The leave campaign seized on the story, warning that the development would undermine NATO and Britain's own security, despite insistence from figures including Philip Hammond, the Foreign Secretary, that the UK would never take part in such a plan (and indeed had vetoed similar pro-posals in 2011).

Nobody in our focus groups had previously heard that an EU army was on the cards, though some said they could well believe it: "If you look at where we've gone from a common market to where we are now, the shape of cucumbers, the threat of an EU army is quite logical. The way things have progressed and moved on." It seemed to most to be a novel idea, and not a very good one: "How would it work? What would it be defending us from?"; "How could the EU have its own army when countries have their own armies and so many have different views?" But for these very reasons, the warning seemed contradictory: if such a development would weaken NATO and damage countries' national defence, why would any member want to sign up to it?

They're all in it together

If voters found it hard to choose between arguments that always seemed either complicated and technical or overblown and unbelievable, their instinct, as at a general election, was to try to choose between the people articulating them. For a variety of reasons, this was hardly any easier.

On the evening of Sunday 21 February, the day after Cameron announced the referendum date, Boris Johnson published his weekly *Telegraph* column. After some apparent agonising, he had decided to campaign for Brexit. In doing so, he in effect became the leader of the leave camp, soon eclipsing even Nigel Farage as the most recognisable figure campaigning for British withdrawal.

> *"It's more of a leadership battle in the Conservative Party than anything else."*

With David Cameron heading the remain effort, this meant the Tories were dominating both sides of the debate. For some who had always voted for other parties, this was disconcerting. They often said that the campaign felt like a continuation of what they saw as the perpetual Conservative Euro-feud, into which the whole nation had now been unwillingly dragged: "It's in the Tory DNA. It goes on all the time. In the Tory party it's been forty years of two camps." It was evident to them that Cameron had only reluctantly agreed to hold the referendum because of pressure from his own MPs, which proved the case.

Since the campaign had become a battle of personalities as well as ideas, it soon began to look to some voters "more of a leadership battle in the Conservative Party than anything else". Though pro-Brexit ministers went out of their way to insist they wanted Cameron to stay even if he lost, most voters agreed with Ken Clarke's assessment that the PM "wouldn't last thirty seconds" if the UK voted to leave. The prospect of engaging in what looked like a prolonged public Tory leadership battle was doubly off-putting, especially to traditional Labour supporters (and triply so in Scotland, where the debate looked to many like a squabble between a particular type of Englishman): "When I see a choice that involves David Cameron, BoJo and Nigel Farage, I think, 'That's a choice that doesn't involve me.'"

As ever, Johnson made his presence felt. After President Obama remarked during his April visit that the UK would be at the "back of the queue" for signing a trade deal with the US, the outgoing Mayor of London wrote an article for *The Sun* reminding readers that Obama had removed from the Oval Office the bust of Winston Churchill which had been presented to his predecessor, George W. Bush. "Some said it was a snub to Britain," Johnson concluded. "Some said it was a symbol of the part-Kenyan President's ancestral dislike of the British Empire – of which Churchill had been such a fervent defender." The article provoked outrage in some quarters. Shadow Chancellor John McDonnell accused Johnson of "dog-whistle racism", assorted columnists denounced him, and the student union at Kings College London withdrew an invitation to take part in a referendum debate on campus.

The undecided voters in one of our focus groups were shown the article, to see if they would be equally scandalised. There was a long silence, during which people looked thoughtful, in the way people do when they think they must be missing something. "…And?" someone asked at last. It was explained that the reference to the President's heritage had caused a stir. "But he is part-Kenyan, isn't he?" Yes, his father was from Kenya. "So what's the problem? Does Obama not want people to know he's part-Kenyan?" If Boris had been provocative, the reaction was out of all proportion: "He's stating a fact, but he didn't need to. But it's not a thing at all. It's just Twitter trying to make something out of nothing."

A few weeks later he was at it again, this time comparing the European Union's ambitions to those of Hitler. Though they were using "different methods", he said in an interview with the *Telegraph*, they shared the aim of uniting Europe under one "authority".

This time, several in our groups had heard about the ensuring row. Some who were not sure of the details but knew Hitler had come into it somewhere feared the worst ("He didn't do one of those salutes, did he?"), and a few who were aware of the substance thought the comparison had been in poor taste: "He's talking about people who wanted to rule the world and sent people to gas chambers." But, again, most of our participants did not think the remarks justified the fuss that followed them. His argument was quite persuasive for some, and certainly a valid one to make: "He was alluding to the fact that people have tried to amalgamate Europe many times, and this is another version of it." As for the rumpus,

"Seriously, Hitler was someone in history and we shouldn't pussyfoot about it."

"The only explanation I can think of is that he can see an angle for himself, to get a foothold to get the top job if Cameron goes."

Though voters recognised him as a powerful advocate (or, at least, publicist) for the Brexit cause, many wondered why he had decided to join it ("The whole thing with Boris is a bit iffy, isn't it?"). Well into the campaign, people in our groups remarked that "Boris was undecided until a couple of weeks ago". Why, they wondered, had he decided to campaign to leave the EU, a position he had never previously argued for? "The only explanation I can think of is that he can see an angle for himself, to get a foothold to get the top job if Cameron goes"; "One has to be a little bit sceptical about Boris's motivations"; "Cameron's position would be untenable. That's why Boris is doing it – opportunism." Some were more prepared to give him the benefit of the doubt: "I think he's put his neck on the line when he didn't need to. But you can never tell with Boris, can you?" If people doubted his motives, so they wondered how sincere he was in the arguments he was making: "He could easily be on the other side himself. It's a pantomime."

Despite the assumption that Cameron would go in the event of a vote for Brexit, the leave campaign never tried to turn the debate into a referendum on the PM himself. If this was a deliberate strategic decision, it was a wise one. In our groups throughout the campaign, nobody thought getting rid of Cameron was a good reason to vote to leave the EU – indeed, the prospect of his departure was enough to make some potential leavers think twice about their decision. For one thing, the country was "going to have to put up with the

Tories" until Labour sorted itself out – for the foreseeable future, in other words – which meant they were looking at the Conservative alternatives to Cameron. Several even thought it would be unfair for him to have to resign if he lost, though they thought it inevitable that he would: "He has given people the democratic right to choose. I think it would be anti-democratic to remove him if the country voted for him last year."

Among Labour voters, any cheers about the possibility of ousting a Tory Prime Minister were therefore shortlived: "Then it will be George Osborne, and that's even more worrying." Alternatively, "We'll be left with Boris, God help us." Would that be so bad? "Oh, God yeah, he's an absolute pillock ... I don't know if the rest of the world would take us seriously"; "He's a politically correct Donald Trump." This view of Johnson was not universal. Many thought very highly of him: "a really intelligent, bright guy who plays the media game but he answers questions very well and articulately and has a knack of being at one with people". But there was a widespread feeling that his popular touch, though impressive and extremely unusual for a politician ("people queue to get his autograph – he's almost a celebrity"), was not a match for the times: "I don't think being a people person is enough at this point. We're talking about jobs for the next fifty or a hundred years, the economy, immigration, the whole culture."

If Boris Johnson had mixed motives when it came to the referendum, he was not, voters felt, the only one. A month before polling day, Steve Hilton claimed that Cameron would be a Brexit supporter were it not for his position: "If he were a member of the public or a backbench MP, or a junior minister or even a cabinet minister, I'm certain he would be for leave," Hilton told *The Times*. Our undecided voters were not sure what to make of this, but even if it were true, some felt, it did not necessarily reflect badly on him: "Relationships get formed, deals get done, handshakes are made and your position can change once you're in the hot seat." But the claim underlined the point that Cameron was fighting not just for his principles but for his job, and so was George Osborne. Did they really believe, then, that Brexit would bring the apocalyptic consequences they predicted every day? Of all the main party leaders, only Nigel Farage seemed to have taken a principled position and stuck to it (though, to be fair, in nine weeks of research nobody mentioned Tim Farron or the Liberal Democrats).

"Nicola Sturgeon is obviously hoping Scotland vote yes and England vote no so she has an excuse for another referendum."

Even Nicola Sturgeon seemed to have an agenda of her own. In our Glasgow groups, most knew the SNP supported remain and the rest assumed it did, but none could recall hearing the First Minister explain why. What they did think they had clocked, however, was that she seemed to see the EU debate first and foremost as a route to re-opening the question of independence: "She's not saying, 'This is why we should stay.' She's obviously hoping Scotland vote yes and England vote no so she has an excuse for another referendum." If she had understandably been consumed by the Holyrood elections for the early part of the campaign, people wanted a stronger lead from her than they thought they had been getting: "She's the leader of this country so her opinion and views should really count for something."

As far as the undecided voters in our focus groups throughout the country were concerned, the biggest absence of all was that of Jeremy Corbyn. Every week, people told us Labour in general, and its leader in particular, were "conspicuous by their absence". Some could not understand why he seemed to be keeping so quiet. He "could be significant, but for some reason he isn't"; "He's been rubbish. He's left it to Alan Johnson. But he's the leader of the Labour Party – he ought to say a bit more than he is"; "For what Labour stand for, especially rights for working people, they should be flying the flag, but they seem to be behind things at the moment."

"Jeremy Corbyn has been rubbish. He's left it to Alan Johnson. But he's the leader of the Labour Party – he ought to say a bit more than he is."

Many others thought they knew the reason for his low profile – that, despite his declared support for remaining in the EU, his heart was not in it. He said was voting to stay "but he doesn't agree with it. He argued for thirty years that we should leave." As late as June, some of our undecided voters were saying that "he hasn't made up his mind. He hasn't come out and said 'I want to stay', at least that I've heard."

Those who had heard him speak on the subject often thought he sounded equivocal ("He finally came out with something today. Although it was a very veiled message, because he said some very pro-Brexit things as well"). Asked in a BBC interview how strongly he felt that Britain ought to remain in the EU on a scale of one to ten, he replied, "Seven, seven and a half," which was, depending on outlook, "grudging" and "half-hearted", or measured and realistic, better reflecting the way voters themselves saw things than the hysterical absolutes emerging from the two campaigns: "He said you might not think everything is perfect about the EU but on balance it's healthier to be in … It's closer to the way I think."

Some remarked that other Labour figures seemed to be

making more of an effort – notably Alan Johnson and Gordon Brown, whose occasional forays were well received ("He does do a good speech, that man"), even if they reminded some that he "sold all the gold and virtually ruined us". But for many Labour voters, these were second-tier voices in the campaign – the lack of a strong, clear lead from the Labour Party meant people were having to "rely on folks like Farage and Boris Johnson that we would otherwise discard like an old jumper".

Though many thought the cross-party nature of the campaign was a good thing in principle, in practice some found it confusing and even worrying. Faced with politicians from different parties arrayed on the same platform, particularly for the remain campaign, what they saw was not so much a constructive alliance of rivals coming together in the national interest as a cosy stitch-up by an establishment trying to protect its own interests: "Those types are all a bit samey. I think of the politics of London, they all went to the same school." Some also found the spectacle seemed inauthentic. Shown a picture of Cameron at an event with Sadiq Khan, the Labour Mayor of London, one of our participants said: "When I saw this I completely tuned out because I couldn't get over how set up and staged the whole thing was. I don't know if it's just David Cameron but I just can't take the whole thing seriously. I don't feel any honesty coming through."

"It's interesting that the Labour leadership are annoyed about it. You can share a platform with Hamas but not with Cameron!"

This question did not arise for Jeremy Corbyn himself, who refused to campaign alongside any Conservatives and was reported to be annoyed with Khan for having appeared with the Prime Minister. This struck some in our groups as rather odd:

"It's interesting that the Labour leadership are annoyed about it. You can share a platform with Hamas but not with Cameron!"

If left-leaning voters were sometimes put off by the impression that "the leave lot are all kind of right wing", the fact that the campaign to stay in the EU was also being led by a Conservative hardly made the choice easier: "If I voted to remain, it would feel odd voting with the leader of the Tory party." And if, as Labour figures intermittently claimed, EU membership was good for such things as workers' rights, the fact that so many Tories backed it too made them wonder if they were missing something: "Cameron supporting remain worries me, actually. I think, 'Why are you in favour?'" At a campaign event at Stansted Airport, Labour stalwart Ed Balls was advocating a remain vote, but who was that sinister character on his right? Wasn't it the one "in charge of the money, the one who brung in the bedroom tax"?

> "If I voted to remain, it would feel odd voting
> with the leader of the Tory party."

The final downside of having to make a political decision without the help of clear party labels, voiced less often but undoubtedly there, was that it was simply harder work: "It's highly complex, life is very busy. You've got to be really in-depth and understand the nitty-gritty ... You need to know more about politics to vote in this than you do in a general election. Then you can vote as your family did, or because of your background, but with this it's not that simple because we've never done it before." Or, to put it another way: "Usually I'd say, 'What do the Tories want?' and do the opposite, but you can't even do that."

CSI Brussels

Instead, as referendum day neared, voters set about the task of judging the case on the available evidence. Our poll[15] in May helps explain how people approached it. Where did the burden of proof lay? Slightly more said the onus was on the leave campaign than on remain – since, as we heard in our groups, people felt the advocates of Brexit were proposing the bigger change to the status quo – but nearly two thirds thought the two sides had an equal responsibility to convince them.

The two competing themes of the campaign were "control" on the one hand and "risk" on the other, and both were powerful. More than six in ten agreed that *we must have more control over our own affairs even if that means missing out on some of the benefits of co-operating with other countries.* Nearly two thirds thought the benefits of membership no longer justified the loss of autonomy they entailed, or never had; or feared too much control would be given away if Britain stayed in the union.

> *"Brexit could be like getting a tattoo when you're young. When you get older, you might regret it."*

At the same time, a small majority said they thought leaving the EU was a bigger risk than remaining (or, as someone in our groups observed, "Brexit could be like getting a tattoo when you're young. When you get older, you might regret it"). Despite the leave campaign's warnings of what the union could become, most thought *the fact that we don't know for sure what life outside the EU would be like* sounded like a bigger risk than *the fact that we don't know for sure how the EU will develop*

15. Lord Ashcroft Polls, EU referendum survey, 13–18 May 2016, sample 5,009.

or change if the UK remains a member – especially to women, younger people and, crucially, undecided voters. Overall, a four-point majority said *the risks to the UK if we make the wrong decision* was likely to play a bigger part in their voting decision than *the importance of controlling our own affairs*.

Yet, when we repeated our exercise from the previous December and asked people to place themselves on a hundred-point scale, where zero meant they would definitely vote to remain and one hundred meant they would definitely vote to leave, 52 per cent put themselves in the upper half, meaning they were leaning towards Brexit, up from 47 per cent five months earlier. More striking still, opinion on the leave side of the scale had hardened. Nearly half of Brexit-inclined voters (which is to say, nearly a quarter of the total) now put themselves at exactly one hundred, meaning they were certain to vote to leave, up from one third in our previous survey. Only one in ten remain-inclined voters – only 4 per cent of the whole – put themselves at the opposite extreme.

To continue the courtroom metaphor, just over half of voters said they would decide *on the balance of probabilities* rather than *beyond reasonable doubt*. By a two-to-one margin, voters aged twenty-four and under said they expected *factual information* to play a bigger part in their voting decision than their *instincts about which is the right decision to take*. This surely reflected the optimism of youth, since most others, and older voters especially, knew that instinct would end up mattering more.

"I just can't understand the issue. With a referendum
I think it needs to be something really quite simple,
like in Ireland when they had gay marriage.
You kind of believe in that one or you don't."

Among the many words people in our groups used to describe the campaign ("unreliable", "unrealistic", "uninformative", "not that interesting", "a quagmire", "a lot of bullshit"), by far the most common was "confusing". Some had even come to resent the whole process: "We should never have had a vote. It's too complex. I just can't understand the issue. With a referendum I think it needs to be something really quite simple, like in Ireland when they had gay marriage. You kind of believe in that one or you don't."

Earlier in the campaign, many of our participants really seemed to hope that they would be given the "facts" that would help them towards a decision – that the "lightbulb moment" would arrive, or that one side would produce a "rabbit from the hat" and make everything clear. As the weeks went by, this hope matured for some voters into the realisation that there were simply no facts to be had: "Do we just need to choose a direction?" This also led to frustration with the two sides' claims to certainty about the future: "In all honesty, how can we know? Why don't they just say, 'This is what we think'?"

But, for many, it curdled into scepticism and, for some, cynicism about practically everything they heard about the referendum. The forecasts of doom had been so relentless that these people had stopped taking them seriously, or even listening. Each side's claims were becoming "ever more extreme", which meant that each new warning about the consequences of making the wrong choice merely added to the "white noise" of the campaign. One even drew a comparison with the millennium bug: "I feel like it's when the year 2000 came and everyone thought the computers would crash and it would be terrible. We woke up the next day and nothing had happened."

*"I feel like it's when the year 2000 came and everyone
thought the computers would crash and it would be terrible.
We woke up the next day and nothing had happened."*

By the end of the campaign, some even began to treat post-Brexit prophecies as an art form. The warning from Donald Tusk ten days before the referendum that British departure could herald the end of "Western political civilisation in its entirety" was admired as a particularly fine example of the genre ("That's pretty good going, isn't it? That's some claim").

Even the most soberly delivered analysis of the potential effects of Brexit began to be dismissed as "scaremongering" (to the annoyance of others who saw this is as merely an excuse not to engage). Though both sides were thought to be guilty of the charge, the blame was not distributed equally. Asked in a YouGov poll[16] two weeks before referendum day which side had *done the most scaremongering*, more than four in ten named the remain campaign (labelled throughout by its opponents as "Project Fear"); 28 per cent thought the opposite.

*"Cameron shouldn't be saying it will be doom and gloom.
He should say there will be life after, but I'd prefer to stay."*

Nor were many people inclined to exonerate either side on the grounds that their words had been over-hyped by the media. If Boris used an historical allusion which prompted the media to compare the EU to Hitler, and if a Cameron speech about national security led the papers to exaggerate and talk about war, they knew what they were doing: "They'd rather get the front page. They were both happy." It need not have

16. YouGov poll, 9–10 June 2016, sample 1,671.

been like this, people thought. A more measured, balanced approach would have been more enlightening: "Cameron shouldn't be saying it will be doom and gloom. He should say there will be life after, but I'd prefer to stay."

Nevertheless, the campaign was over and the decision was upon them. This was "one time only", "a bigger deal than a general election" and "a proper dilemma"; "I swing so much between the two. I have actually got butterflies." As the gap in the polls narrowed, few in our groups of undecided voters concurred with Nigel Farage's observation that people were using the referendum to "put two fingers up to the political class". However much people agreed with the sentiment, especially after the campaign they had just endured, there was too much at stake for that: "This is real life. It's real money and it affects real people."

APPENDIX TO CHAPTER III

The following results are from our 5,000-sample poll conducted one month before the referendum, in May 2016.

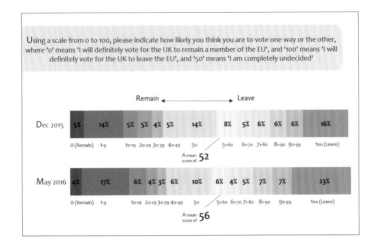

Using a scale from 0 to 100, please indicate how likely you think you are to vote one way or the other, where '0' means 'I will definitely vote for the UK to remain a member of the EU', and '100' means 'I will definitely vote for the UK to leave the EU', and '50' means 'I am completely undecided'

Remain ← → Leave

Dec 2015 | 5% | 14% | 5% | 5% | 4% | 5% | 14% | 8% | 5% | 6% | 6% | 6% | 16%

0 (Remain) 1-9 10-19 20-29 30-39 40-49 50 51-60 61-70 71-80 81-90 90-99 100 (Leave)

A mean score of **52**

May 2016 | 4% | 17% | 6% | 4% | 3% | 6% | 10% | 6% | 4% | 5% | 7% | 7% | 23%

0 (Remain) 1-9 10-19 20-29 30-39 40-49 50 51-60 61-70 71-80 81-90 90-99 100 (Leave)

A mean score of **56**

Which of the people on the leave side have done the best job of putting across their argument?

Boris Johnson was named spontaneously by 1,707 respondents – more than four times as many as the next most mentioned campaigner, Nigel Farage (358). Michael Gove received 219 mentions, Iain Duncan Smith 104, David Cameron 41 and Donald Trump 40.

Which of the people on the remain side have done the best job of putting across their argument?

David Cameron dominated the remain side, with 1,248 mentions. Both President Obama (199) and Mark Carney (187) were mentioned more often than Jeremy Corbyn (144). Gordon Brown (79) was named more often than George Osborne (54).

Arguments heard from the leave campaign (open-ended):

Arguments heard from the remain campaign (open-ended):

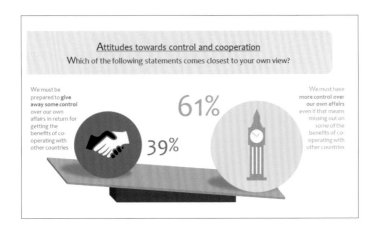

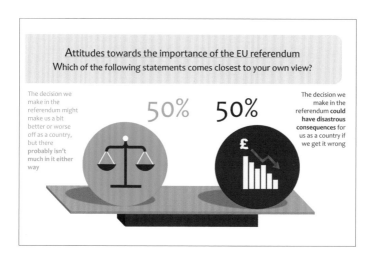

Attitudes towards the importance of the EU referendum
Which of the following statements comes closest to your own view?

The decision we make in the referendum might make us a bit better or worse off as a country, but there probably isn't much in it either way

50%

50%

The decision we make in the referendum **could have disastrous consequences** for us as a country if we get it wrong

IV. WHAT HAPPENED AND WHY

On Thursday 23 June, 16,141,241 people voted for the UK to re-main in the European Union. 17,410,742 people voted to leave. At 72 per cent, turnout was higher than for any UK-wide ballot since the 1992 general election.

As the polls closed, YouGov published their final survey of the campaign. Having returned to five thousand people who took part in their penultimate poll the previous day, they projected a victory for remain by 52 to 48 per cent (the mirror image of the result that came to pass). The earliest returns, from Sunderland and Newcastle, showed higher shares for leave than had been expected. The trend continued – Scotland, Northern Ireland and London were the only three regions in which a majority voted to remain – and by four in the morning the broadcasters were ready to project that the country had voted for Brexit. Shortly after eight, David Cameron an-nounced his resignation as Prime Minister.

On referendum day, Lord Ashcroft Polls conducted a sur-vey,[17] online and by telephone, of 12,369 people after they had voted. The results help explain who voted for which outcome and, more importantly, why. One in ten of our participants – in other words, some three million voters – only decided how to vote on the day itself, or on the day they filled in their postal vote. Overall, nearly a quarter made their mind up in the final

17. 'How the United Kingdom voted… and why', LordAshcroftPolls.com.

week of the campaign; they divided fairly evenly between the leave and remain camps, illustrating the lack of a late swing to the status quo. Just under half of voters (43 per cent) said they had always known how they would end up voting, or had decided more than a year before the referendum – again, this group did not heavily favour one side or the other.

Who voted how

Stats

There were clear demographic differences between leave and remain voters. Nearly three quarters (73 per cent) of those aged eighteen to twenty-four voted to remain, while a majority of those aged over forty-five voted to leave. Six in ten voters aged sixty-five or above backed Brexit. More than half of those on a private pension voted to leave, as did two thirds of those retired with only a state pension.[18] Most of those with children aged ten or under voted to remain; most of those whose children were aged eleven or older voted to leave.

Professionals and managers (often described as the 'ABs') were the only social group among which a majority (57 per cent) voted to remain. The white-collar 'C1' group leaned towards leaving by two points. Nearly two thirds of skilled manual workers ('C2s'), and of unskilled manual workers and those dependent on state benefits, voted for Brexit. Overall, those currently working voted to remain by a four-point margin. Most university graduates, nearly two thirds of those with

18. This divergence of opinion between age groups excited a good deal of comment to the effect that old people had deprived the young of their desired future, until evidence emerged that most young people had not bothered to vote. BBC analysis based on census figures showed that the higher the proportion of young people in an area, the lower the turnout. Analysis by Sky News estimated that just 36 per cent of voters aged under twenty-four had voted in the referendum.

a postgraduate degree and four in five of those still in full-time education voted to stay in the EU; among those whose formal education had ended at secondary school, 64 per cent voted to leave.

Among voters in private rented accommodation there was a ten-point lead for remain, and there was an eight-point remain lead among voters with mortgages. Those who owned their homes outright voted to leave by a ten-point margin. Around two thirds of council house and housing association tenants voted for Brexit.

While white voters elected to leave by a six-point margin, two thirds of those describing themselves as Asian voted to remain, as did three quarters of black voters. Nearly six in ten of those identifying themselves as Christians voted to leave; seven in ten Muslims voted to remain. (The sample sizes for other faiths were too small to draw firm conclusions – though 70 per cent of the eighty Hindus who responded to the poll had voted to stay, and 54 per cent of the ninety-eight Jewish voters who took part had voted to leave.)

When it came to party allegiance, the picture was more mixed. A majority (58 per cent) of those who voted Conservative at the 2015 general election voted to leave the EU. Just under two thirds (63 per cent) of Labour supporters voted to remain, as did seven in ten Liberal Democrats and three quarters of Greens. Scottish National Party voters backed remain by nearly two to one – or, to put it another way, since Scotland's First Minister, Nicola Sturgeon, would use Scotland's support for EU membership as the basis to seek a second referendum on Scottish independence, nearly half (44 per cent) of Scottish support for Brexit came from her own SNP supporters.

Reasons to remain, reasons to leave

In our poll we asked people to rank, in order of importance to their eventual voting decision, four statements that encapsulated the main arguments of each campaign. On both sides, Conservative and Labour voters put the statements in the same order of priority.

Remain

(1) For remain voters, the single most important reason for their choice, ranked first by 43 per cent of them, was that *the risks of voting to leave the EU looked too great when it came to things like the economy, jobs and prices.* Conservative voters were the most likely to choose this argument; 49 per cent of them said it was the most important.

(2) Just over three in ten (31 per cent) said the strongest argument was that *a vote to remain would still mean the UK having access to the EU single market while remaining outside the euro and the no-borders area of Europe, giving Britain the best of both worlds.* (3) More than one in six (17 per cent) feared above all that *by leaving the EU, the UK would become more isolated from its friends and neighbours.* (4) Fewer than one in ten remain supporters (9 per cent) said they had voted to continue Britain's membership because of *a strong attachment to the EU and its shared history, culture and traditions.* Green voters (16 per cent) were the most likely to name this as the most important reason for their vote.

Leave

(1) Among leave voters, the biggest single reason for wanting to leave the EU was *the principle that decisions about the UK should be taken in the UK.* Nearly half (49 per cent) of all leave voters said this was the most important argument for Brexit, including a majority of ABs, Conservatives and Lib Dems who voted for withdrawal. (2) This point about sovereignty outweighed even the feeling that *voting to leave the EU offered the*

best chance to regain control over immigration and its own borders, which was chosen as the main reason by one third of all leavers (including 39 per cent of UKIP voters, compared to 27 per cent of Conservatives who voted to leave).

(3) Just over one in eight leavers said their main motivation had been the fear that remaining did not mean sticking with the status quo, but *having little or no choice about how the EU expanded its membership or its powers in the years ahead.* Only just over one in twenty (6 per cent) said their main reason for voting to leave was that *when it comes to trade and the economy, the UK would benefit more from being outside the EU than being part of it.*

Further evidence of how the claims and themes from either side ultimately played out came from our analysis of which side had the better of each issue, and how closely each was correlated with people's ultimate voting decisions. We gave people a list of fifteen issues and asked whether each was more likely to be better if the UK remained a member of the EU, or left. Despite the overall majority for Brexit, each side had seven of the issues to its advantage; on one, *our protection against terrorism*, people were precisely divided.

On most economic issues, the remain camp had slim leads. By four points, people thought *economic security for you and your family* would be better if we were to remain, as would *job prospects* (by two points, though three quarters of 18–24-year-olds thought this), *the economy as a whole* (by five points), *the cost of living* (by ten points) and – a rather less slender advantage – *investment in the UK by international companies* (by twenty points). By a very narrow two-point margin, people also thought remaining would be better when it came to *opportunities for children growing up today* and, by eight points, *the UK's influence in the world*. As these numbers imply, not all of those who thought there were economic benefits to remaining voted to do so: one in ten leavers thought job prospects and personal economic security would be better inside the EU; one in six thought the same about the cost of living, and a quarter thought EU membership would attract more foreign investment.

Three themes dominated the list of issues on which the leavers had the advantage: *border controls* and *the immigration system*, both of which people thought would be better outside the EU by margins of forty points, and *the ability to control our own laws*, on which there was a 56-point gap. Eight in ten Conservatives and more than half of Labour and Lib Dem voters thought immigration and border control would be better if the UK were to leave, as well as a majority of eighteen to twenty-fours and nearly four in ten remainers; a clear majority of all groups, not to mention 44 per cent of those who voted to remain, thought the country would be better able to control its own laws after Brexit. By narrower margins, voters as a whole thought things would be better outside the EU when it came to *fairness in the welfare system* (by fourteen points), *rights for people in the UK* (by ten points), *the NHS* and *the quality of life in the UK* (both by six points).

Two nations?

The starkest differences between leave and remain voters were not in their demographic characteristics or even their usual political allegiances, but in their social attitudes and general view of the world. These explain at least as much about why people voted as they did as the direct arguments for and against EU membership – indeed, they probably explain more.

In England, there were marked differences in view according to how people saw their national identity. The relatively small proportion of the population who described themselves as "English not British" (12 per cent) voted to leave the EU by 79 to 21 per cent. UKIP voters were twice as likely as the general population to identify themselves in this way. Meanwhile, those who considered themselves more British than English voted to remain by nearly two to one. To look at the question from the other end, leavers were twice as likely as remainers to feel more English than British; more than twice as many remainers as leavers felt more British than English.

There was also some correlation in Northern Ireland, where leavers were more likely than remainers to describe themselves as British rather than Irish or Northern Irish. In Scotland, the effect was less marked: just under half of leavers (46 per cent) and just over half of remainers (55 per cent) identified themselves as Scottish rather than British. In Wales, there was no discernible relationship between people's referendum vote and the strength of their feeling of Welshness.

Those who were less politically engaged were more likely to vote for Brexit. Among those who admitted they paid little or no attention to politics, 58 per cent voted to leave; those who said they paid a great deal of attention divided evenly. It is also notable that most (54 per cent) of those who voted to leave expected the remain side to win – either because the polls and the odds on the day pointed to that outcome or because, when it came to politics, many were not used to getting their own way.

Leavers were notably more pessimistic, both about the country and about their own prospects in it, than those who voted to remain. Majorities in both groups agreed that *if you work hard, it is possible to be very successful in Britain no matter what your background*, though remainers did so by a bigger margin (and half of UKIP leavers, and most Labour leavers, thought it truer to say that *in Britain today, people from some backgrounds will never have a real chance to be successful no matter how hard they work*). But, while a small majority of remainers agreed that *for most children growing up in Britain today, life will be better than it was for their parents*, leavers thought that for most British children *life will be worse than it was for their parents*, by a 22-point margin. By 71 to 29 per cent, leavers agreed that *with the way the economy and society are changing, there will be more threats to my standard of living in future than there will be opportunities to improve it*; remainers agreed by half this margin.

Perhaps most tellingly of all, nearly three quarters of those who voted to remain in the EU agreed that *overall, life in Britain today is better than it was thirty years ago*, as did 57 per cent of all voters. By contrast, nearly six in ten leavers, including 70 per cent of UKIP supporters, thought that *overall, life in Britain today is worse than it was thirty years ago*.

The two groups' attitudes to various aspects of modern life confirm the point. Seven in ten of those who thought multiculturalism a force for good voted to remain; eight in ten of those who thought it a force for ill voted to leave; there was a similar story on immigration. Six in ten of those who thought feminism had been a good thing voted to stay; nearly eight in ten of those who thought the opposite voted to go. Most of those who believed the green movement had been beneficial voted in; seven in ten of those who thought it had not voted out. Seven in ten of the admittedly small number of people who considered the internet a force for ill opted for Brexit.

Well, you did ask

Several things are clear from all this. One is that, as foreshadowed in our focus groups throughout the campaign, a sizeable number of voters embraced Brexit even though they thought this might involve an economic cost. They placed more importance on other matters: reducing immigration and, above all, feeling that they – or at least the people they elected – had control over the things that affected their lives.

This does not necessarily mean that the heavy focus on the economy amounted to a strategic mistake on the part of the remain campaign. This was their strongest suit and, as we have seen, the most persuasive of the arguments they advanced. An appeal to the spirit of internationalism and the European ideal would have made little headway.

Why, then, did these warnings of economic disaster not carry the day? One reason, for which our research offers plenty of evidence, is that the foretellings of doom sounded so overblown that people decided to take them with more than a pinch of salt. Added to that, the leave campaign did a good enough job of neutralising the remain advantage on the economy. They were able to mobilise enough business supporters to contest the idea of a consensus that the UK was better off in, and however hotly disputed their £350 million figure, they successfully conveyed the idea that membership came at colossal cost. In doing so, and by preventing the runaway leads on economic issues that the remain camp had banked on, the leave side succeeded in making the risks and rewards of Brexit feel much more balanced. Many felt there might be some economic disruption, but that this would probably be shortlived and would, in any case, be a price worth paying to be free of the EU.

But there is more to it than that. Whatever the economic rewards of EU membership were supposed to be, millions of people were not feeling them, while being all too aware of what they saw as its drawbacks. Someone was probably benefiting from it all, they thought, but whoever it was, it wasn't them. If the members of the gilded elite who daily admonished them of the risks were as scared as they claimed to be, that was probably because they had the most to lose. As we also found in our referendum-day poll, while more than three quarters of remain voters thought the decision *could have disastrous consequences for us as a country if we get it wrong*, more than two thirds of leavers thought whatever path we took *might make us a bit better or worse off as a country, but there probably isn't much in it either way*.

Above all, whatever was printed on the ballot paper, the question large numbers of voters heard, and the reply they gave, was nothing much to do with the European Union. People tried to wrestle with such facts as were available, and to make sense of the competing promises and claims. But, ultimately, the question many saw was: "Are you happy with the way things are, and the way they seem to be going?" And their answer was: "Well, since you ask… no."

The full consequences of these newly exposed divisions will take some time to become clear. Some predict a political realignment along the lines of "open" and "closed" rather than left and right, reflecting – they argue – the two kinds of political outlook present in the British electorate. But, as we have seen, "the 52 per cent" and "the 48 per cent" were themselves coalitions of voters, some of whom had little in common with each other apart from the box they ticked on 23 June – just as the same is true among those who voted for any given party thirteen months earlier. The novelty of the referendum was not so much the forces it supposedly unleashed but that it removed the party structure through which political opinions are usually expressed.

Party loyalties still exist, though they are becoming ever looser, and may well have been weakened further by the referendum and its aftermath. As well as securing Britain's withdrawal from the EU on the best possible terms, it now falls to the new Conservative Prime Minister, Theresa May, to keep together the Tory-voting coalition David Cameron assembled in 2015 – remain and leave alike. At the same time, with previously solid Labour voters having declined to take their party's lead in the referendum, her opposition counterpart must prevent what happened to Labour in Scotland at the 2015 election being repeated in the Midlands and the North of England. That is the way our voting system works. Unless, of course, we want to have another referendum to change it.

APPENDIX TO CHAPTER IV

The findings on pages 122–4 are from our 12,000-sample referendum-day poll of people who had cast their vote.

Published polls on UK membership of the EU: 2010 to 2016

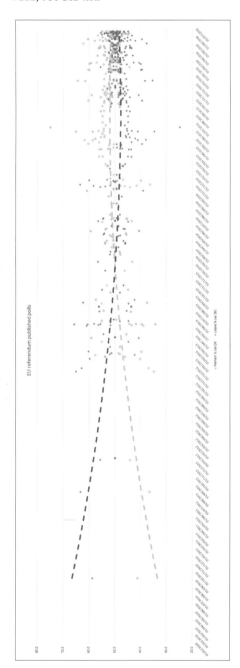

EU referendum published polls

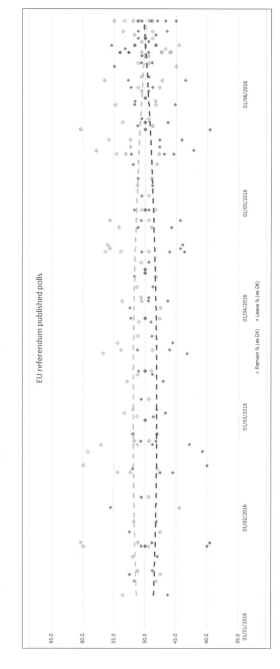

Published polls on UK membership of the EU: January to June 2016

EU referendum published polls

◇ Remain % (ex DK)   ◆ Leave % (ex DK)

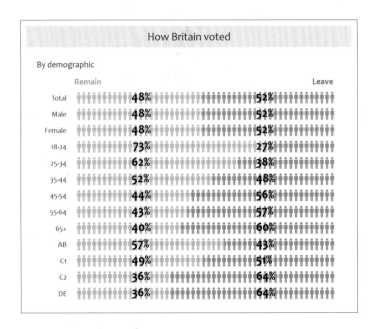

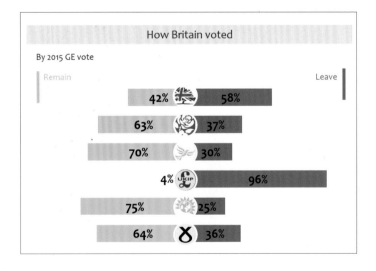

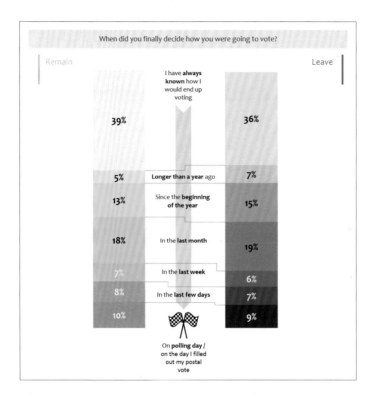

When did you finally decide how you were going to vote?

Remain | Leave

I have **always known** how I would end up voting
39% | 36%

Longer than a **year** ago
5% | 7%

Since the **beginning of the year**
13% | 15%

In the **last month**
18% | 19%

In the **last week**
7% | 6%

In the **last few days**
8% | 7%

On **polling day** / on the day I filled out my postal vote
10% | 9%

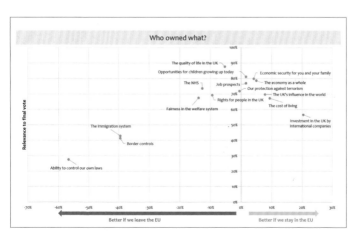

Who owned what?

Relevance to final vote

The quality of life in the UK
Opportunities for children growing up today
Economic security for you and your family
The NHS
Job prospects
The economy as a whole
Our protection against terrorism
The UK's influence in the world
Rights for people in the UK
The cost of living
Fairness in the welfare system
Investment in the UK by international companies
The immigration system
Border controls
Ability to control our own laws

Better if we leave the EU | Better if we stay in the EU

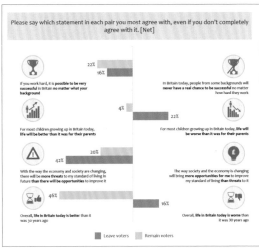

Maps, charts and graphics have been produced with the help
of The Noun Project and AMCHARTS.

Full details of Lord Ashcroft's political research can be found at
LordAshcroftPolls.com. You can also follow him on Twitter: @LordAshcroft.